FOOTBALL, DREAMS & OBSTACLES

CHANDRA GUPTA

"To achieve greatness in football, you must never stop learning and acquiring knowledge. The more you know about the game of football, the better prepared you'll be for whatever challenges come your way."

Chandra Gupta

TABLE OF CONTENTS

Part-1

How to become a better football player (all factors)"

INTRODUCTION / PREFACE

Dear readers,

Football is a sport that brings the world together. People from different backgrounds and cultures come together to play and watch this amazing game. I fell in love with football when I was very young, playing with passion and dedication. My name is Chandra Gupta, and I'm a football lover turned author.

As a child, I dreamed of becoming a professional footballer. Sadly, societal pressures led me down a different path, and I became an author instead. Even though I didn't pursue a football career, my love for the game never faded. I continued to follow football closely, researching and learning about its development in India.

As an author, I wanted to give back to the sport that brought me so much joy. That's why I wrote this book. It's a guide for anyone wanting to pursue a football career, especially in India, where the sport is still growing. I've gathered years of research, knowledge, and passion to help beginners and aspiring footballers achieve their dreams.

This book covers everything you need to start your football journey. From the basics of the game to advanced techniques and strategies, it's all here. I've also included tips on training, nutrition, and overcoming challenges. Whether you're just starting or have some experience, this book has something for everyone.

My goal is to help young players reach their full potential and achieve their dreams of becoming professional footballers. With the right guidance and support, anyone can excel in this sport. I've made this book easy to understand so that everyone can benefit from its insights and advice.

I hope this book becomes a valuable resource for anyone looking to make a career in football. Whether you're a beginner or an experienced player, I hope it inspires and motivates you to achieve greatness. Thank you for reading, and I hope this book helps you on your journey to becoming a successful footballer.

Sincerely,

Chandra Gupta

I am filled with gratitude as I introduce my book, a guide for those passionate about football who want to make a career in this beautiful sport. After researching and understanding the deep infrastructure and system of Indian football, I am proud to have written this book as a perfect guide for beginners and aspiring footballers. This book is the result of my love for the sport and my desire to help others achieve their dreams of becoming successful footballers.

I am thankful for the chance to share my knowledge and experiences with others and to help young players reach their full potential. I believe that with the right guidance and support, anyone can achieve greatness in sports, and that is what this book aims to provide.

While writing this book, I have carefully studied many **research papers** on football **nutrition, sports science, training plans, and routines** to ensure you get the best and most accurate information. Being a **master in psychology**, I have also added important **psychological techniques that are 100% valid and effective**. In addition, I have researched over **200 websites, research papers, authentic news, and reports** to bring you the most reliable and useful content. Although I cannot mention every source by name, I am deeply thankful to all those whose work has helped shape this book.

HOW TO READ THIS BOOK?

This book is a guide for those who love football and dream of making a career in this amazing sport. My goal is to give you a clear understanding of what it takes to become a good footballer and to help you overcome any challenges you might face.

First, keep an open mind and be ready to learn. The information in this book comes from my own experiences and research, but it's just one viewpoint. Make sure to consider other perspectives as you read.

Second, read with a purpose. Think about what you want to learn from this book and set specific goals. This will help you stay focused and get the most out of it.

Lastly, put what you learn into practice. This book is not just about giving you information but also about helping you achieve your goals. Reflect on what you read and think about how you can use it in your life. Whether it's practicing drills, finding more resources, or changing your perspective, the key is to take action.

I hope this book becomes a valuable resource for you and helps you on your way to becoming a successful footballer. With the right approach and mindset, I believe anyone can reach their full potential in this sport. Good luck, and I wish you all the best on your journey!

WHY A FOOTBALL CAREER SHOULD BE A GOAL FOR SOMEONE.

Dreaming to become a footballer can give your life purpose and motivation. Football, or soccer, is loved by millions of people around the world, and for good reason. It's a game that needs a mix of skill, physical fitness, and mental toughness. It also can bring people together, connect with their emotions, and create memories that will last a lifetime.

One of the best things about football is its simplicity. At its core, it's just a game played with a ball, but the complexity and beauty of the sport come from the way it can be played in so many different ways. Whether it's a casual pickup game with friends or a high-stakes match in front of thousands of fans, the game can be enjoyed by people of all ages and skill levels.

For many people, football is more than just a game—it's a passion. The sport has the power to evoke a wide range of emotions, from the thrill of a last-minute game-winning goal to the disappointment of a tough loss. Fans of the game can also connect to it on a deeper level, as they can identify with their favorite players and teams and feel a sense of pride and camaraderie when they succeed.

For aspiring footballers, the dream of becoming a professional player is incredibly motivating. The dedication and hard work required to achieve that dream can help instill valuable life skills such as discipline, perseverance, and teamwork. And for those who make it to the professional level, the rewards can be immense, both in terms of financial compensation and the sense of accomplishment that comes from achieving one's goals.

Football also has a unique ability to unite people from different backgrounds and cultures. The sport has the power to bring together people from all over the world and create a sense of community and belonging. Football matches can be a place where people come together to celebrate their shared love for the game, regardless of their differences.

Having a dream of becoming a footballer can be incredibly powerful and motivating. Football is a sport that is beloved by millions of people around the world, and it has the ability to bring people together and connect with their emotions. Aspiring footballers can gain valuable life skills and a sense of accomplishment from working towards their dreams, while fans can find joy, passion, and a sense of community. Whether you're a player, a coach, or a fan, football has the power to make a positive impact on your life.

WHY SPORTS SCIENCE IS VERY IMPORTANT IN FOOTBALL

Sports science plays a very important role in football for many reasons:

Injury Prevention: Sports science helps reduce the risk of injury by improving players' fitness, diet, and training methods. This helps players stay healthy and perform at their best.

Performance Improvement: Sports science improves players' performance by creating training programs that match their specific needs and strengths. This helps players become faster, stronger, and more agile on the field.

Recovery: Sports science helps players recover from injuries more quickly and effectively. This includes making recovery plans, using special equipment and methods, and monitoring their progress to ensure they fully heal.

Tactical Analysis: Sports science helps coaches and players study and understand their opponents' strategies and ways of playing. This information can then be used to create better game plans.

<u>Data-Driven Decisions:</u> Sports science provides information based on data that helps coaches and players make better decisions. This includes tracking performance, watching for injuries, and studying tactics.

Sports science is important in football because it helps to improve performance, reduce injury risk, and provide useful information for making decisions. This leads to a more successful and safe experience for players and teams.

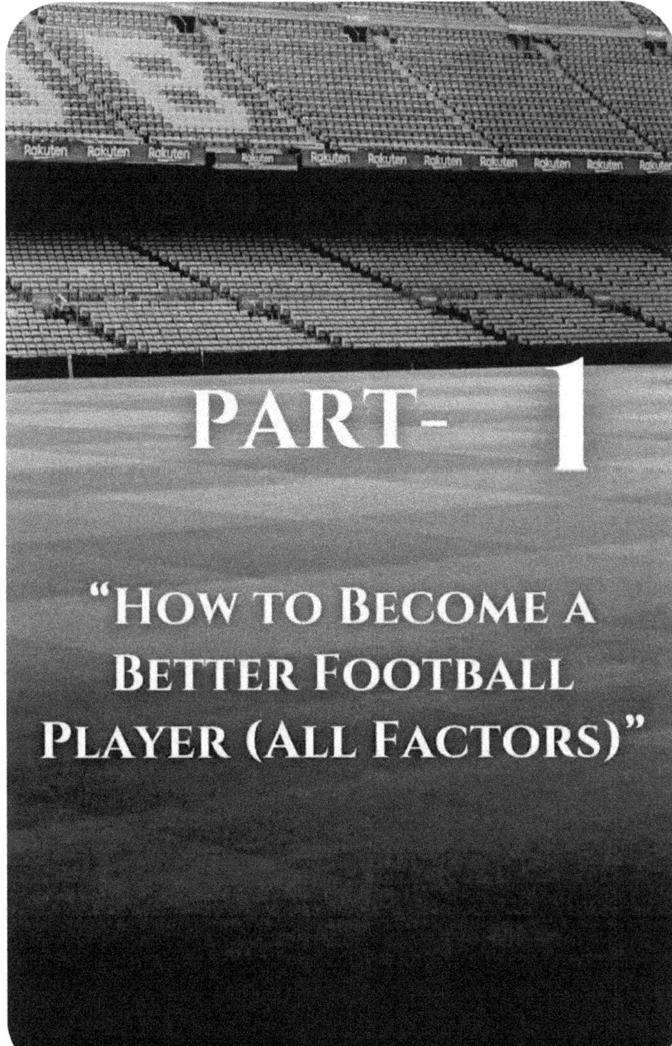

PART- 1
"HOW TO BECOME A BETTER FOOTBALL PLAYER (ALL FACTORS)"

CHAPTER – 1

Positive Attitude

Being a good football player means having a positive attitude. This means facing challenges with a "can-do" attitude, optimism, and determination. Players with a positive outlook are better at overcoming problems and staying motivated during tough times. They perform better on the field, work well with teammates, recover from setbacks, become mentally strong, and are more willing to learn from coaches. This leads to more resilience, focus, and teamwork. Players with a positive outlook are more likely to keep trying hard and reach their full potential. By approaching games and practice with a positive attitude, players set themselves up for success.

Football success relies a lot on having a positive attitude. It impacts the whole team and improves the player's performance. A positive outlook helps boost motivation, resilience, teamwork, and confidence. Confident football players are more likely to take risks and make bold moves that could win the game. Teamwork is very important in football, and a positive attitude makes it easier for players to get along. On the field, when players are positive and support each other, communication and coordination improve. This means they are more likely to trust and rely on one another.

Players will face setbacks and challenges in their careers, and resilience is key to overcoming these difficulties. When players have a positive attitude, they are less likely to focus on their mistakes and more likely to learn from them and move on. Motivation is also very important in any sport, and a positive attitude helps players stay motivated even when things get tough.

When players believe in their ability to succeed, they are more likely to work hard and push themselves to improve, which leads to better performance on the field. Having a positive attitude is very important for any football player. It helps them succeed in their efforts. A positive attitude leads to success on and off the field because it improves player performance and creates a positive and supportive team environment.

How to Be Positive

To develop a positive outlook as a football player, consider these suggestions:

Focus on Now: It's easy to worry about past mistakes or what might happen in the future, but staying focused on the present helps you stay balanced and do your best.

Be Thankful: Appreciate the chances and experiences you have as a football player. Think about the things you are grateful for, like the opportunity to play, your team's support, and your own skills.

Set Realistic Goals: Goals help you focus your energy and motivation. Make sure your goals are clear, measurable, and achievable. Celebrate your progress as you reach each goal.

Be Around Positive People: Surround yourself with upbeat and motivating individuals. Find positive role models and teammates who share your positive outlook.

Stay Positive During Tough Times: Football is both physically and mentally challenging, so it's easy to lose motivation. Focus on what you can control and take positive steps.

Talk to Yourself Positively: Your thoughts greatly influence your feelings and actions. Make sure your inner dialogue is positive and supportive.

Take Care of Your Body: Good physical and mental health are important. Get enough sleep, eat healthy, and stay hydrated.

Remember, developing a positive attitude takes time and effort. Be patient and persistent. Surround yourself with positive influences and focus on your progress, not just your mistakes. With practice, you can develop a positive attitude that will help you perform your best on the football field.

"A positive attitude on the football field is like a superpower, it gives you the strength to overcome obstacles, the courage to try new things, and the determination to succeed."

Chandra Gupta

CHAPTER – 2

Consistency

Being consistent is very important for improving as a football player. Consistency means being able to perform well at a high level all the time. A consistent player is someone you can rely on to play well throughout the game.

Here's why consistency matters in football:

Better Performance: When a player is consistent in their training and playing, their skills usually get better. By regularly putting in the effort to train and practice, a player will improve their abilities, gain confidence, and perform better in games.

Building Confidence: Consistently playing well on the field helps build a player's confidence. When a player feels sure that they can always perform at a high level, they are more likely to try new things and take risks on the field, which can lead to even better performances.

Trust from Coaches and Teammates: If you are consistent, your coaches and teammates will trust you more. Coaches and teammates are more likely to rely on a player in important moments and give them more playing time if they are confident that the player will deliver good performances regularly.

Mental Toughness: Consistency also requires mental strength. A mentally tough player can keep playing well even when things get tough or distracting. This mental strength is a big advantage on the field because it helps a player stay focused and perform well, even in challenging situations.

There are several ways to play consistently in football:

Regular Practice: The key to getting better at football is practicing regularly. Players should make sure they attend training sessions often and work hard to improve their skills.

Proper Nutrition: Eating a healthy, balanced diet helps a player perform at their best. Good nutrition provides the energy and nutrients needed for top performance on the field.

Rest and Recovery: Resting and recovering are important for consistency. Players should make sure they get enough sleep and recover from injuries to avoid a drop-in performance.

<u>**Mental Preparation:**</u> Being mentally prepared is also important for consistency. Players can train their minds to stay focused and perform well under pressure, which helps them stay mentally strong.

Being consistent is key to becoming a better football player. Regular practice, healthy eating, rest and recovery, and mental preparation all help improve consistency. A consistent player can be relied on to perform well, earn the respect of coaches and teammates, and maintain their strong form.

"Consistency in football is like the heartbeat of success, it keeps you on track, drives your passion, and propels you towards greatness."

—Chandra Gupta

CHAPTER – 3

Dedication and Hard Work

To be a good football player, you need to be dedicated and work hard. Football is a tough sport, both physically and mentally, and it takes years of training and practice to master the skills needed to play at the highest level.

If you want to succeed as a football player, you must be committed to your craft. This means spending the necessary time and energy to improve your skills, both on and off the field. It may require long training and practice sessions, and sometimes you might have to give up other things in your life to focus on football.

Hard work is also essential in football. Whether you're practicing your dribbling, shooting, or tackling, you must be willing to put in the effort to get better. This includes attending extra training sessions, watching game footage, and evaluating your performance to identify areas where you can improve.

Other factors can help you improve your football skills too. It's important to have a strong work ethic, a positive attitude, and the ability to learn from your mistakes. You should also be physically fit, with a healthy diet and a regular exercise routine that helps you build strength and endurance.

Having a strong support system is another important part of football success. This can include family, friends, and coaches who believe in you and support you. Being in a positive and encouraging environment can help you stay motivated and committed to your goals, even when things get tough.

Becoming a good football player takes a combination of dedication, hard work, and natural talent. It's not an easy path, but with persistence and determination, you can succeed and become one of the best players on the field. Whether you're just starting or already have some experience, stay focused, keep working hard, and never give up on your dreams.

How to Achieve Dedication and Hard Work Toward Football:

Becoming a good football player takes more than just talent—it also requires dedication and hard work. Here are some simple tips to help you stay committed and improve your skills in the field:

Set clear Goals: Having clear goals will help keep you motivated and focused. Write down your short-term and long-term goals, and track your progress.

Stay Focused: Avoid distractions and stay focused on your practice and games. Keep discipline in your life and stay away from habits that could harm your performance, like smoking or excessive drinking.

Train Regularly: Regular practice is key to getting better. Set aside time each day to work on specific skills or drills. Also, make sure to practice often with your team to improve coordination and teamwork.

Watch and Learn from the Pros: Study how professional players play the game to learn new strategies and techniques. Watch their games, and pay attention to their moves, decisions, and tactics.

Get Enough Sleep and Eat Right: Getting enough sleep and eating healthy are important for staying strong and focused. Aim for 7-8 hours of sleep each night, and eat a balanced diet with plenty of protein, carbs, and healthy fats.

Keep a Positive Attitude: Stay positive even when things don't go your way. Believe in your abilities and focus on what you can control, rather than getting stuck on setbacks.

Ask for Feedback: Ask your coaches, trainers, and teammates for feedback to find out where you can improve. Be open to learning from your mistakes and keep trying to get better.

Embrace Positive People: Surround yourself with people who support and inspire you. A strong support system can help keep you motivated and focused on your goals.

<u>**Remember to Have Fun:**</u> Football is a game, and it should be fun. Don't take yourself too seriously—enjoy the journey of learning and growing as a player.

Remember, becoming a good football player takes time and effort. Stay positive, work hard, and keep your dreams in mind as you train and play. With dedication and determination, you can reach your goals and become a better player.

CHAPTER – 4

Good Coaching in Football

<u>**Good coaching is really important for football players to reach their best potential. Here's why:**</u>

Skill Development: A good coach helps players improve their skills like dribbling, shooting, and passing. They teach the right drills and exercises to build these skills and give feedback to make players even better.

Understanding of Tactics: Coaches help players understand the game better, including tactics and strategies. They teach about different formations, how to play in different positions, and why movement off the ball is so important.

Mental Preparation: Football isn't just physical—it's mental too. A good coach helps players stay focused and mentally strong. They teach players how to manage their emotions, overcome challenges, and stay motivated.

Physical Development: Coaches also focus on improving players' physical abilities like strength, endurance, and speed. They create training programs to build these skills and help players recover from injuries.

Building Confidence: Confidence is key in football. Good coaches encourage players, set realistic goals, and give them chances to succeed, helping to build their confidence.

Teamwork: Since football is a team sport, a good coach teaches the importance of working well with others. This includes communication, cooperation, and trust on the field.

Adaptability: Coaches help players learn to adapt to different situations. This includes understanding different systems and styles of play and adjusting to different opponents and conditions.

Preparation: Being well-prepared is crucial. Good coaches develop game plans, provide information about opponents, and help players get in the right mindset for games and training sessions.

Game Intelligence: Game intelligence means understanding the game deeply, knowing the strengths and weaknesses of opponents, and making smart decisions during play. A good coach helps players develop this ability.

Personal Growth: Beyond the field, a good coach helps players grow as people. They guide players in setting personal goals, offer support, and help them reach their full potential.

Good coaching is the foundation for a player's success in football. A coach who focuses on skills, tactics, mental and physical preparation, confidence, teamwork, adaptability, and personal growth can make a huge difference in helping players achieve their goals and become better players.

Tips for Finding the Best Football Coach:

Finding the right coach can make a big difference in how you grow as a football player. Here's how you can find the best coaching to help you reach your full potential:

Do Your Research: Start by looking for local coaches, programs, and football academies. Check for coaches who have successfully developed players before. Ask current or former players for their recommendations.

Check Coaching Style: Pick a coach whose style matches how you like to learn. Watch how the coach works with players. Notice how they talk to and motivate their players.

Look for Experience: Find a coach who has a lot of experience in playing and coaching football. An experienced coach will understand the game better and can help you improve faster.

Ask for a Trial: Before making a final decision, ask if you can attend a few sessions to see if the coach is right for you. Pay attention to how the coach gives instructions, the feedback they provide, and how the training sessions feel.

Get Feedback from Others: Talk to other players or parents who have worked with the coach. Their opinions can give you a better idea of the coach's style and how effective they are.

Build a Good Relationship: Once you find a coach you like, it's important to have a good working relationship. Talk openly with your coach, and ask for regular feedback on how you're doing.

Be Ready to Learn: The most important thing is to be willing to learn. Listen carefully to what the coach says, ask questions if you don't understand, and work hard to apply their advice.

Take Charge of Your Growth: While the coach will guide you, it's up to you to work hard and focus on your improvement. Stay committed to getting better every day.

<u>**Keep Checking Your Progress:**</u> Regularly think about how your coaching is going. Make sure you're making progress and getting the support you need. If you're not happy with the coaching, don't be afraid to look for another coach.

Finding the right coach is key to your success as a football player. Do your homework, check your options, and choose a coach who can help you reach your goals. With the right coach and a lot of hard work, you can become a better player.

CHAPTER – 5

<u>Technical skills</u>

Football players need strong technical skills to do well on the field. These skills include controlling the ball, making good passes, and doing different moves like dribbling, shooting, and tackling.

A player with good technical skills can control the ball better, pass more accurately, and make precise moves during the game. This helps the player perform better and make smarter decisions while playing.

Having good technical skills is also important when playing under pressure. A player's technical ability often decides the outcome in tough situations, like when the game is close.

Players also need strong technical skills to adapt to different game situations. Whether playing against a strong defense or trying to get past a defender, good technical skills give players the tools to succeed.

To improve their technical skills, players need to practice regularly. This can include individual drills, small games, and working with a coach to focus on specific areas that need improvement.

Technical skills are a key part of being a good football player. With strong technical skills, players can control the ball better, improve accuracy, and handle pressure. To reach their full potential, players must keep practicing and training their technical skills.

Here are some tips to help you get better at football:

Practice often: The more you practice, the better you'll get. Spend time every day working on ball control, dribbling, shooting, and passing.

Watch pro players: Pay attention to how professional players move. Look at how they use their feet, position their bodies, and make decisions on the field.

Master the basics: Before trying advanced skills, make sure you're good at the basics like ball control, dribbling, and passing.

Improve your dribbling: Dribbling is very important in football. Practice using both feet, and try dribbling at different speeds and with different moves.

Focus on ball control: Being able to control the ball is key. Practice trapping the ball with different parts of your body and work on controlling it while you're on the move.

Get better at passing: Passing is a big part of football. Practice passing with both feet, and work on making your passes accurate and at the right speed.

Work on your shooting: Shooting is how you score goals. Practice shooting from different spots on the field, using different parts of your foot, and changing the speed and angle of your shot.

Build speed and agility: Being fast and agile is important. Do drills that help you get quicker and more agile on the field.

Learn from a coach: Joining a team or working with a coach can help you improve. A coach can give you tips and feedback to help you reach your goals.

Prepare mentally: Getting your mind ready is just as important as getting your body ready. Picture yourself doing the skills you're working on, and focus on the steps you need to take rather than just the end result.

CHAPTER – 6

Tactical knowledge

Tactical knowledge is very important for football players to understand the game and make good decisions on the field. When players know the tactics well, they can predict what their opponents might do and react in the right way. This helps the team work better together and increases the chances of winning.

Tactical knowledge means knowing how to read the game and make quick decisions. For example, some common tactics in football include the pressing game, counter-attacks, and formations like 4-4-2. It's also about understanding what each position on the field does, like what a full-back, center-midfielder, or striker should do.

Another part of tactical knowledge is knowing how to handle different situations during a match. This could mean defending a lead, trying to score when behind, or playing against a team that has more players on the field. Knowing what to do in these situations helps players make smart choices and do their jobs better.

Having strong tactical knowledge is key for any player who wants to reach their best potential. It allows them to make good decisions, work well with teammates, and help their team succeed. A player who understands tactics well will be able to adjust to different situations and always play at a high level.

Here are some simple steps to help you improve your tactical knowledge in football:

Learn About Formations: Get to know different football formations like 4-4-2, 3-5-2, and 4-3-3. Think about how each formation changes the way a team plays. Some formations may help with attacking more, while others may make the defense stronger.

Watch Players Closely: Pay attention to what each player does on the field and how they fit into the team's plan. This will help you understand why positions like central midfielders, defenders, and forwards are so important.

Read About Tactics: There are lots of books, articles, and websites that talk about football tactics. Reading them can help you understand the strategies and methods used by the best teams.

Learn from Coaches: If you can, take lessons or work with a coach who can teach you about tactics and give you feedback. This will help you understand the ideas and techniques you've learned from other sources.

CHAPTER – 7

<u>Understanding of the game</u>

To be a great football player, it's important to truly understand the game. This means knowing the rules, tactics, and strategies that make football what it is. When you understand these things, you can make smart choices on the field, perform your skills better, and predict what your opponents might do next. This kind of understanding helps you see where the game is going, adjust to changes, and react quickly to surprises.

It's also important to understand the mental and emotional side of football. Players need to stay calm under pressure, keep a positive attitude, and manage their emotions. You can do this by building mental strength and knowing your own strengths and weaknesses.

Having a good understanding of the game also helps you communicate better with your teammates. When you can talk to each other clearly, you can plan your moves, work together to reach your goals, and build trust. This is very important for teams because the best teams are often the ones that understand the game and each other's strengths and weaknesses the best.

A deep understanding of football helps players make good decisions, communicate well, and perform well under pressure.

Here are some simple tips to help you understand football better and become a better player:

Learn the Rules: Make sure you know all the basic rules of football, like offside, fouls, and corner kicks. This will help you play the game the right way.

Think Like a Footballer: Good players think ahead and make quick decisions. Try to imagine the game in your mind and practice making fast choices on the field.

Work as a Team: Football is all about working together. Understand your role in the team and make sure you and your teammates are working towards the same goal.

Know Your Position: Every position has its own job. Learn what your position requires and work on the skills that are important for it.

Look at Your Own Game: After each match, take some time to think about how you played. Find areas where you can get better and work on those.

<u>**Listen to Your Coach:**</u> Be open to feedback from your coach. They have lots of experience and can help you improve.

<u>**Enjoy the Game:**</u> Football is a fun sport. The more you enjoy playing, the more you'll learn and get better. Play with passion and have fun on the field.

CHAPTER – 8

<u>Mental strength in football</u>

Football players need mental toughness to play their best and handle challenges under pressure. A player's mental toughness helps them stay motivated, focused, and confident even when things get tough.

To build mental strength, players should work on being resilient and confident while managing their emotions and stress. This means keeping a positive attitude, focusing on strengths, and learning from mistakes. A mentally tough player can bounce back from failures, stay positive, and perform well when the pressure is on.

Mental toughness is important in high-pressure situations, like penalty kicks or important moments in a game. Players with strong mental toughness handle pressure better, stay focused on their goals, and play with confidence. They are less likely to get flustered or make mistakes, which can often decide the outcome of a match.

In football, quick thinking and split-second decisions are needed, especially during intense moments. Mental toughness helps a player trust their instincts and make the right choices even under stress.

Dealing with setbacks and recovering from injuries also requires mental toughness. Players with strong mental strength stay motivated, keep their eyes on their goals, and work hard to get back to their best. They recover quickly from setbacks and don't let challenges stop them, which is important for long-term success.

Mental toughness helps football players perform at their best and face challenges in high-pressure situations. It supports good decision-making, helps in dealing with setbacks, and keeps players motivated even when things are hard. Developing this toughness is important for any player who wants to play at a high level and contribute to their team's success.

Here are some simple tips to help you build mental strength in football:

Focus on the Process: Instead of worrying about the final result, concentrate on what you can control—your preparation, how you play, and your attitude.

Visualize Success: Imagine yourself doing well in a game. This can help you stay calm, boost your confidence, and perform better when it counts.

Set Realistic Goals: Make sure your goals are achievable, both in the short term and long term. This keeps you motivated and focused.

Practice Mindfulness: Stay present in the moment, especially during high-pressure situations. This helps you remain calm and focused.

Manage Stress: Find ways to reduce stress, like exercising, meditating, or spending time with loved ones. Lowering stress helps you think more clearly.

Bounce Back from Failure: Understand that failure is part of life. Learn from it and see it as a chance to improve. This will help you recover quickly and keep moving forward.

Surround Yourself with Positivity: Stay close to positive and supportive people. Cut out negativity from your life, whether it's from people, social media, or other sources.

Use Positive Self-Talk: The way you talk to yourself matters. Focus on your strengths and what you can do well to build your confidence.

Get Enough Sleep: Make sure you're well-rested. Sleep is crucial for your mental and physical recovery, helping you stay sharp and focused.

Stay Physically Fit: Exercise regularly to boost your mood, reduce stress, and stay in good shape, all of which help your mental performance.

"Mental strength in football is what sets champions apart. It gives you the resilience to overcome challenges, the focus to stick to your game plan, and the willpower to keep going when your body says stop."

— Chandra Gupta

<u>Good nutrition and football</u>

Good nutrition and a proper diet are very important for a football player's performance and overall health. Eating the right foods gives players the energy and nutrients they need to stay in good shape and play their best on the field.

Football players should eat a diet rich in protein and carbohydrates. Protein helps build and repair muscles, while carbohydrates provide energy. These nutrients also help players recover quickly after hard training and games. Drinking plenty of water is also essential because it keeps the body cool, prevents cramps, and helps both the body and mind stay sharp.

A balanced diet with lots of vitamins, minerals, and antioxidants is important for a strong immune system, which helps protect against illness and injury. Players should aim to eat a variety of fruits and vegetables, whole grains, lean proteins, and healthy fats to get all the nutrients they need.

It's also important for football players to pay attention to their nutritional needs and avoid unhealthy diets or skipping meals. Diets that are too restrictive or unbalanced can lead to poor nutrition, low energy, and bad performance on the field.

Football players who eat well and maintain a healthy diet have the energy and nutrients they need to perform at their best, recover quickly, and reduce the risk of injury and illness. By understanding their nutritional needs and sticking to a balanced diet, players can reach their full potential and contribute to their team's success.

Here are some simple tips to help football players get the right nutrition:

Eat Enough Calories: Football requires a lot of energy, so players need to eat enough food to keep up with their training and games. The amount of calories needed depends on things like age, weight, and how active you are.

Stay Hydrated: Drinking enough water is very important for playing well. Players should drink plenty of fluids before, during, and after practices and games to avoid getting dehydrated. Sports drinks with electrolytes can also help replace the salts and minerals lost through sweat.

Balance Your Meals: Football players need a good balance of carbs, protein, and fats. Carbs give you energy, protein helps build and repair muscles, and fats provide extra energy and help your body absorb vitamins.

Get Enough Protein: Protein is important for muscle growth and repair, especially after hard physical activity. Make sure to include enough protein in your diet to support your body's needs

Choose Complex Carbs: Complex carbs, like those found in whole grains, fruits, and vegetables, provide energy that lasts longer. These are better for keeping your energy up during games and practices.

Limit Junk Food: Processed foods often have too much sugar, salt, and unhealthy fats, which can hurt your performance and recovery. Try to eat more whole, nutritious foods instead.

Eat at the Right Time: When you eat is just as important as what you eat. Before a game or practice, have a meal or snack with carbs and protein to give you energy. Afterward, eat something similar to help your body recover.

Keep Your Energy Up: On practice or game days, it's important to eat and drink enough to keep your energy up. Eating small meals and snacks throughout the day can help you stay fuelled and avoid feeling too full.

By following these tips, football players can get the nutrition they need to stay strong, perform well, and recover quickly.

CHAPTER – 10

Physical fitness

Any football player who wants to play their best on the field must be physically fit. A fit player can control their body better, keep up their energy throughout the game, recover faster from injuries, and perform skills more accurately.

Physical fitness in football includes strength, power, speed, agility, and endurance. A football player needs all of these to do things like sprinting, jumping, tackling, dribbling, and shooting during a game.

Strength helps players push off opponents and stay strong in challenges.

Power allows them to accelerate quickly and change direction on the field.

Speed and agility help them outrun opponents and get to the ball first.

Endurance is needed to play the entire 90 minutes without getting tired or making mistakes.

Being physically fit also reduces the chance of getting hurt. A fit body handles the demands of the game better, and good balance and coordination help players avoid falls and collisions.

Physical fitness isn't just about exercise; it's also about eating well and staying hydrated. Eating enough protein and carbohydrates helps with recovery and performance while staying hydrated is key to avoiding cramps and staying focused.

To stay fit, football players need to practice regularly and include both strength and cardio training in their routines. Along with skill practice on the field, this will help keep their fitness levels high.

Physical fitness plays a big role in how well a football player performs. A fit player will have better control, more energy, fewer injuries, and sharper skills. By combining regular training with a healthy diet and staying hydrated, football players can reach their full potential.

<u>Being physically fit is key to being a good football player. To get there, you need to focus on a few important areas:</u>

<u>Aerobic Endurance:</u> Football requires a lot of running, sprinting, and jogging throughout the game. To keep up your performance, you need strong aerobic endurance. To improve this, include long-distance running and interval training in your workouts.

<u>Strength and Power:</u> Football players need to be strong and powerful for activities like tackling, jumping, and running. You can build strength and power by adding weightlifting, plyometrics, and other resistance exercises to your routine.

<u>Speed and Agility:</u> Speed and agility are crucial in football because they help you change direction and make quick movements on the field. To improve, do drills and exercises that focus on quick footwork and coordination.

<u>Flexibility and Balance:</u> Being flexible and balanced is important for movements like jumping, turning, and sliding. Stretching should be a part of your warm-up and cool-down routines to improve flexibility. To improve balance, work on exercises that strengthen your core and stability.

<u>Nutrition:</u> Good nutrition is vital to support your fitness goals as a football player. Eat a balanced diet rich in protein to help muscles grow and repair, complex carbohydrates for energy, and healthy fats for overall well-being.

"Physical fitness in football is like the foundation of a building. It gives you the strength to handle pressure, the agility to change direction, and the stamina to play at full speed from start to finish."

— Chandra Gupta

CHAPTER – 11

Regular practice and training

To get better as a football player, you need to practice and train regularly. Football is both physically and mentally demanding, so it takes a lot of commitment.

Here's why practicing and training often is important for football players:

Building Skills: Football needs a lot of different skills, like dribbling, passing, shooting, and defending. When you practice regularly, you get better at these skills and become more confident on the field.

Gaining Strength and Endurance: Football is a tough sport that requires players to be in good shape. Regular training helps you build strength and stamina, so you can play your best throughout the game.

Learning Team Tactics: Football is a team game, so it's important to understand your team's strategies. By practicing often, you learn how your team plays and where you fit in, which makes you more effective and confident on the field.

<u>Improving Teamwork and Communication:</u> Football requires players to work closely together and communicate well. When you train with your team regularly, you learn how to work better together, understand each other's strengths and weaknesses, and communicate clearly.

<u>Mental Readiness:</u> Football is also a mental game that requires focus and discipline. Regular practice helps you build mental toughness, so you can stay calm and perform well under pressure.

<u>Preventing Injuries:</u> Football has a risk of injury, especially if you're not well-prepared physically. Regular practice improves your technique and lowers the chances of getting hurt by reducing risky moves.

<u>Staying Motivated:</u> Consistent practice and training help you stay motivated and focused on your goals. It lets you see your progress and gives you a sense of achievement.

Becoming a good football player takes a lot of practice and training. It helps you build your skills, gain strength and stamina, learn team tactics, improve teamwork and communication, prepare mentally, prevent injuries, and stay motivated. Football players who train regularly have a much better chance of succeeding on the field.

"Regular football practice is like watering
the seeds of success. It nourishes your skills,
sharpens your technique, and helps you
reach your full potential on the field."

— Chandra Gupta

CHAPTER – 12

Understanding the Opponent

In football, knowing your opponent is very important if you want to win. It helps players guess what the other team will do and change their game to match. To be a good football player, you need to understand and study the other team.

One big advantage of knowing your opponent is that you can guess what they might do next. This helps you to get into the right position and make the right move, whether you're defending or attacking. For example, if you know your opponent likes to dribble towards the goal or make long passes, you can be ready to block them or cut off their pass.

Another important part of understanding your opponent is knowing their strengths and weaknesses. If you know what your opponent is good or bad at, you can adjust your play to take advantage. For instance, if they are not good at defending in the air, you might focus on making more high passes or crosses. If they are fast and make quick runs, you can change your strategy to slow them down.

Understanding your opponent isn't just about tactics; it also affects your confidence. When you know your opponent's strengths and weaknesses, you feel more confident, and it might even make your opponent nervous, leading them to make mistakes.

To really understand your opponent, you need to practice, watch them play, and think about what you see. Watching them during a game helps you notice their habits, strengths, and weaknesses. Then, you can break down what you saw and figure out the strategies they use. Finally, you can use this information during the game to take advantage of their weaknesses and play to your strengths.

One of the best ways to understand your opponent is to watch videos of their games. By doing this, you can learn more about how they play and use that knowledge to improve your own game.

Understanding your opponent is a key part of becoming a good football player. It helps you guess their moves and adjust your game plan. By watching, thinking, and practicing, you can learn more about your opponents and use that knowledge to play better and more successfully.

"Understanding your opponents in football
is like studying your enemy in battle. It
gives you the insight to guess their moves,
the knowledge to take advantage of their
weaknesses, and the edge to win the game."

— Chandra Gupta

CHAPTER – 13

<u>Teamwork</u>

To be a successful football player, good teamwork is really important. A football team has 11 players, and while each one has their own special skills, winning games happens when everyone works together as a team.

The first and most obvious benefit of good teamwork is that it helps players work together to reach a common goal. In football, the main goal is to score goals and win matches. To do this, players need to coordinate their moves and actions on the field, working together to outsmart the other team and create chances to score.

Good teamwork also builds trust and strong bonds between players. When players trust each other, they are more likely to play well together, both on and off the field. This trust can lead to better performances because players feel confident in each other's abilities. When players are close to one another, they also support and encourage each other, especially when things are tough. This can help keep everyone's spirits high and focused on the game.

Communication is a big part of good teamwork in football. In any team sport, talking to each other is key because it helps players plan their moves and make quick decisions. This is especially true in football, where success often depends on making the right choice at the right moment. When players communicate well, it also reduces mistakes and confusion because everyone knows what they need to do.

Good teamwork can also lead to better individual performances. When team members work well together, they can use each other's strengths to their advantage. For example, a striker might score more goals if their teammates create good opportunities for them. Similarly, a defender might make more tackles and interceptions if they can count on their teammates to help cover and support them.

In football, good teamwork means players work together to reach a common goal, build trust, communicate well, and improve each other's performance. When a team can create a strong sense of unity and work well as a group, they are much more likely to win games and achieve their goals.

"Teamwork in football is like a symphony of success, where each player adds their unique skills to create a beautiful and powerful performance on the field."

— Chandra Gupta

CHAPTER – 14

Adaptability

To be the best football player you can be, you need to know how to adapt. Football is a game that's always changing, so players have to be ready to handle different situations on the field. Whether it's dealing with sudden problems like injuries or weather changes, or adjusting to a new position or the other team's tactics, being able to adapt is key to becoming a good football player.

Adaptability requires both mental and physical skills. Mentally, players need to be quick thinkers who can understand what's happening during the game and come up with smart solutions. Physically, they need to be able to change how they move, control the ball, or where they position themselves on the field to adjust their play.

Players who are open to change and willing to try new things are more likely to be adaptable. This could mean learning new skills that might be outside of their comfort zone or becoming more flexible and versatile as a player. It's also important for players to work hard and be ready to put in the time and effort to develop the skills they need.

The ability to adapt is a must for any football player who wants to do well. Whether you're a beginner or have been playing for years, your success on the field depends on how well you can handle different situations and challenges. By working hard and building the skills you need, you can become the best football player you can be.

Here are some tips to help you become more adaptable on the football field:

Watch and Learn: One of the best ways to get better at adapting is to watch other football players. Pay attention to how your favorite players handle different situations during a game. Notice how they change their tactics when the game changes and try to use those ideas in your own play.

Practice Different Scenarios: During training, practice different situations you might face in a game. This could mean playing against different types of opponents or trying out different strategies and formations. The more you practice these, the more comfortable you'll be when you face similar situations in a real game.

<u>Be Open-Minded:</u> Being open to new ideas is important for adapting well. Be willing to try new things and listen to feedback from your coach and teammates. This will help you adjust to new situations and keep improving your game.

<u>Communicate with Your Teammates:</u> Good communication with your teammates is key to being adaptable. Make sure to talk with them about the strategies you want to use and ask for their thoughts. This will help you work together as a team and respond to changes in the game more effectively.

"Adaptability in football is like being a chameleon on the field; it lets you blend in with the game's changing situations and come out on top no matter what challenges you face."

Chandra Gupta

CHAPTER – 15

Good Time Management

To be a good football player, you need to manage your time well. Being a football player means you have to balance your time between training, playing, and other important things in your life. Good time management helps you focus on what's important, use your time wisely, and avoid getting distracted.

There are several reasons why managing your time well is important. First, it helps you make sure you have enough time for practice and training, which are essential to improving your skills and performance. Second, it allows you to balance your football responsibilities with other important things, like work or school, which can affect how well you play.

Third, good time management keeps you motivated to play football and helps prevent burnout. It also helps you manage the physical demands of playing football, like making sure you get enough rest and recovery time. This is important for avoiding injuries and staying in top physical shape.

To improve your time management skills, you should create a schedule and stick to it. This might mean setting aside specific times for training, practice, rest, and recovery, as well as other responsibilities like work or school. You should also try to limit the time you spend on distractions, like social media or video games.

Managing your time well is key to being a good football player. It helps you focus on training, balance your other responsibilities, avoid burnout, and stay physically fit. By mastering time management, you can reach your full potential and become a top football player.

Here are some easy tips to help you manage your time well:

Set Goals: Start by setting clear and reachable goals for your football career. Write down what you want to achieve in the short, medium, and long term. Having clear goals will keep you motivated and focused.

Plan Your Day: Make a daily schedule that includes time for training, games, rest, and recovery. Don't forget to plan time for healthy eating, enough sleep, and taking care of your body and mind.

Prioritize Your Tasks: Focus on the most important tasks first. For example, if you have a big game coming up, spend more time on training and recovery so you can perform your best.

<u>Stay Organized</u>: Use a planner or an app to keep track of your schedule and to-do list. This will help you stay on top of things and avoid missing important deadlines or appointments.

<u>Learn to Say No</u>: It's okay to say no when you need to. If something isn't important or might get in the way of your training or recovery, it's okay to pass on it.

<u>Use Your Free Time Wisely</u>: Make the most of your free time by doing things that help you reach your goals. For example, you could read books or watch videos about football to learn more about the game.

<u>Stay Focused</u>: Keep your eyes on your goals and try to avoid distractions. Stay away from things like social media or other activities that might take up too much of your time and energy.

<u>Rest and Recover</u>: Rest and recovery are just as important as training and playing. Make sure you have enough time to rest and recover to avoid injuries and burnout.

<u>Get Enough Sleep</u>: Getting enough sleep is key to performing well on the field. Try to get at least 8 hours of sleep each night so you're well-rested and ready to play.

<u>Ask for Help</u>: If you ever feel overwhelmed, don't hesitate to ask for help. Whether it's a coach, mentor, or friend, there's always someone who can help you manage your time and stay on track.

"Good time management in football is like keeping the clock on your side. It helps you make the most of your chances, stay focused on your goals, and make sure every moment on the field counts."

-Chandra Gupta

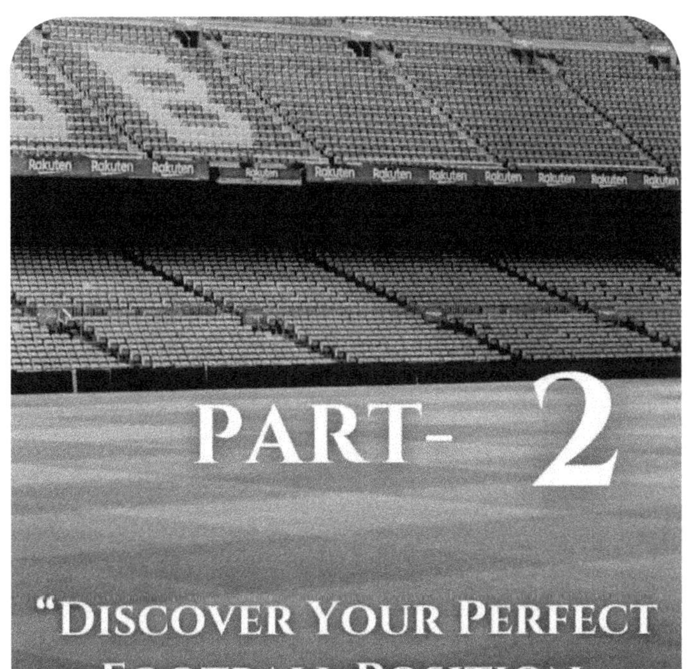
PART- 2
"DISCOVER YOUR PERFECT
FOOTBALL POSITION:
ASSESSMENTS AND
TEMPLATES FOR PLAYERS
OF ALL POSITIONS"

Goalkeeper Test: Find Out If You Can Be a Goalkeeper

Are you wondering if you have what it takes to be a goalkeeper? This simple test will help you figure out if you're a good fit for the position based on your skills and qualities. Let's see if you're meant to be a goalkeeper!

Instructions: Answer each question honestly by picking the option that best describes you. Take your time and think about each question. At the end, add up your points to see if you could be a great goalkeeper.

Questions:

Q. How good are you at stopping shots?

a) I have excellent reflexes and quick reactions.

b) I'm pretty good at making saves.

c) I'm okay at stopping shots.

d) I find it hard to make saves.

Q. What's your best skill in the game?

a) Protecting the goal and catching high balls.

b) Organizing the team and talking to my teammates.

c) Passing the ball quickly and starting attacks.

d) Kicking the ball far or throwing it accurately.

Q. How confident are you in one-on-one situations?

a) I feel very sure and often save shots.

b) I'm a little unsure but can handle some situations.

c) I struggle to save shots in one-on-one situations.

d) I feel overwhelmed and usually can't save shots.

Q. How good are you at reading the game?

a) I'm great at predicting what the other team will do.

b) I'm pretty good at understanding the game.

c) I'm average at guessing what the other team will do.

d) I have trouble figuring out what the other team is planning.

Q. How comfortable are you with passing the ball accurately?

a) I'm very comfortable and pass well with my feet.

b) I'm decent at passing the ball accurately.

c) I struggle to pass the ball accurately.

d) I'm not good at passing the ball with my feet.

Q. Are you a good leader on the field?

a) I'm a natural leader and guide the defense well.

b) I'm comfortable leading and helping my teammates.

c) I prefer to follow rather than lead.

d) I lack confidence in leading the team from the back.

<u>Scoring:</u>

- a) = 4 points
- b) = 3 points
- c) = 2 points
- d) = 1 point

<u>**Check Your Score:**</u>

- **20-24 points:** You could be an excellent goalkeeper. Keep working on your skills!
- **14-19 points:** You show promise as a goalkeeper. Keep practicing and improving.
- **8-13 points:** You have some potential, but you might need to focus on specific areas.
- **6-7 points:** Goalkeeping might not be the best position for you. You might want to try other positions that fit you better.

Remember, this is just a guide to help you explore your potential as a goalkeeper. You can always improve and try out different positions in football!

Template for Footballers: Finding Your Best Defensive Position

1. Center-back Assessment:

Are you thinking about playing as a center-back? This simple test will help you find out if you're a good fit for the position based on your skills and qualities. Let's see if center-back is the right spot for you!

Instructions: Answer each question honestly by picking the option that best matches you. Take your time and think about each question. After you finish, add up your points to see if you're a good fit for being a center-back.

Assessment Questions:

Q. How comfortable are you with winning aerial duels?

a) I'm excellent at winning headers & dominating in the air.

b) I'm pretty good at winning aerial battles.

c) I'm okay at challenging opponents in the air.

d) I struggle to win headers consistently.

Q. How well can you anticipate and intercept passes?

a) I'm exceptional at reading the game and intercepting passes.

b) I'm decent at anticipating and making interceptions.

c) I have an average ability to anticipate and intercept passes.

d) I have trouble predicting and intercepting passes.

Q. How comfortable are you in physical duels and tackles?

a) I feel confident and win physical battles consistently.

b) I can hold my ground and win tackles most of the time.

c) I occasionally struggle in physical duels and tackles.

d) I feel overwhelmed and find it difficult to win physical battles.

Q. How good are you at organizing and communicating with teammates?

a) I'm a natural leader and effectively organize the defense.

b) I can communicate and organize the defense reasonably well.

c) I have an average ability to organize and communicate.

d) I lack confidence in organizing and communicating with teammates.

<u>Scoring:</u>

- a) = 4 points
- b) = 3 points
- c) = 2 points
- d) = 1 point

<u>Check Your Score:</u>

- **12-16 points:** You could be an excellent center-back. Keep working on your skills!
- **8-11 points:** You show promise as a center-back. Keep practicing and improving.
- **4-7 points:** You have some potential, but you might need to work on specific areas.

- **1-3 points:** Center-back might not be the best position for you. You might want to try other defensive positions that fit you better.

---

2. Right-back Assessment:

Are you thinking about playing as a right-back? This template will help you see if you're a good fit for the position based on your skills and qualities. Let's find out if you might be a right-back!

Instructions:

Answer each question honestly by picking the option that best describes you. Take your time with each question. After you finish, add up your scores to see how well you fit as a right-back.

Assessment Questions:

Q. How comfortable are you with making overlapping runs and crossing the ball?

a) I'm great at overlapping and sending accurate crosses.

b) I can overlap and cross the ball well.

c) I sometimes overlap and cross the ball.

d) I find it hard to overlap and cross accurately.

Q. How good are you at defending one-on-one against wingers?

a) I'm really good at stopping wingers and winning one-on-one battles.

b) I can defend well in one-on-one situations against wingers.

c) I'm okay at defending one-on-one against wingers.

d) I struggle to defend against wingers in one-on-one situations.

Q. How comfortable are you with getting back quickly after joining the attack?

a) I'm excellent at tracking back and defending after attacking.

b) I can get back quickly after joining the attack.

c) I sometimes have trouble getting back quickly after attacking.

d) I find it hard to get back on defense after attacking.

Q. How well can you predict and intercept passes in your defensive area?

a) I'm great at reading the game and intercepting passes.

b) I'm pretty good at anticipating and intercepting passes.

c) I'm okay at predicting and intercepting passes.

d) I struggle to predict and intercept passes in my area.

<u>Scoring and Results:</u>

<u>Give yourself points for each answer:</u>

- a) = 4 points
- b) = 3 points
- c) = 2 points
- d) = 1 point

<u>Add up your points to see how well you fit as a right-back:</u>

12-16 points: You're a great fit to be a right-back. Keep working on your skills!

8-11 points: You're a good fit and have potential. Keep practicing!

4-7 points: You have some potential, but you might need to work on certain areas.

1-3 points: Right-back might not be the best position for you. You could explore other defensive roles.

3.Left-back Assessment:

Are you thinking about playing as a left-back? This template will help you see if you're a good fit for the position based on your skills and qualities. Let's find out if you might be a left-back!

Instructions:

Answer each question honestly by picking the option that best describes you. Take your time with each question. After you finish, add up your scores to see how well you fit as a left-back.

Assessment Questions:

Q. How comfortable are you with making overlapping runs and crossing the ball from the left side?

a) I'm great at overlapping and sending accurate crosses from the left.

b) I can overlap and cross the ball well from the left.

c) I sometimes overlap and cross the ball from the left.

d) I find it hard to overlap and cross accurately from the left.

Q. How good are you at defending one-on-one against wingers on the right side?

a) I'm really good at stopping wingers and winning one-on-one battles on the right.

b) I can defend well in one-on-one situations against wingers on the right.

c) I'm okay at defending one-on-one against wingers on the right.

d) I struggle to defend against wingers in one-on-one situations on the right.

Q. How comfortable are you with getting back quickly after joining the attack from the left side?

a) I'm excellent at tracking back and defending after attacking from the left.

b) I can get back quickly after joining the attack from the left.

c) I sometimes have trouble getting back quickly after attacking from the left.

d) I find it hard to get back on defense after attacking from the left.

Q. How well can you predict and intercept passes in your defensive area on the left side?

a) I'm great at reading the game and intercepting passes on the left.

b) I'm pretty good at anticipating and intercepting passes on the left.

c) I'm okay at predicting and intercepting passes on the left.

d) I struggle to predict and intercept passes in my area on the left.

<u>**Scoring and Results:**</u>

<u>**Give yourself points for each answer:**</u>

- a) = 4 points
- b) = 3 points
- c) = 2 points
- d) = 1 point

<u>**Add up your points to see how well you fit as a left-back:**</u>

12-16 points: You're a great fit to be a left-back. Keep working on your skills!

8-11 points: You're a good fit and have potential. Keep practicing!

4-7 points: You have some potential, but you might need to work on certain areas.

1-3 points: Left-back might not be the best position for you. You could explore other defensive roles.

<u>**Remember, this assessment is a guide, and you can continue to grow and explore different positions in football.**</u>

Template for Footballers: Finding Your Best Midfield Position

1. Defensive Midfielder (Holding Midfielder) Assessment:

Are you thinking about playing as a defensive midfielder? This template will help you see if you're a good fit for the position based on your skills and qualities. Let's find out if you might be a defensive midfielder!

Instructions:

Answer each question honestly by picking the option that best describes you. Take your time with each question. After you finish, add up your scores to see how well you fit as a defensive midfielder.

Q. How comfortable are you with intercepting and stopping the opponent's attacks?

a) I'm great at intercepting and stopping opponent's attacks.

b) I'm good at disrupting opponent's attacks.

c) I sometimes succeed in intercepting and stopping attacks.

d) I struggle with intercepting and stopping opponent's attacks.

Q. How good are you at covering for the defense and protecting them?

a) I'm skilled at covering for the defense and protecting them.

b) I can provide some cover and protection for the defense.

c) I sometimes succeed in covering and protecting the defense.

d) I find it hard to provide strong defensive cover and protection.

Q. How well can you pass the ball and start attacks from a deeper position?

a) I'm excellent at passing and starting attacks from deeper positions.

b) I'm pretty good at passing and starting attacks from deeper areas.

c) I'm okay at passing and starting attacks from deeper positions.

d) I struggle with passing and starting attacks from deeper areas.

Q. How comfortable are you with staying in position and reading the game?

a) I'm great at staying in position and reading the game.

b) I'm good at keeping my position and reading the game sometimes.

c) I sometimes manage to stay in position and read the game.

d) I find it hard to stay in position and read the game.

<u>Scoring and Results:</u>

<u>Give yourself points for each answer:</u>

- a) = 4 points
- b) = 3 points
- c) = 2 points
- d) = 1 point

<u>**Add up your points to see how well you fit as a defensive midfielder:**</u>

12-16 points: You're a great fit to be a defensive midfielder. Keep working on your skills!

8-11 points: You're a good fit and have potential. Keep practicing!

4-7 points: You have some potential, but you might need to work on certain areas.

1-3 points: Defensive midfielder might not be the best position for you. You could explore other midfield roles.

---

2. Central Midfielder (Box-to-Box Midfielder) Assessment:

Are you thinking about playing as a central midfielder? This template will help you see if you're a good fit for the position based on your skills and qualities. Let's find out if you might be a central midfielder!

<u>**Instructions:**</u>

Answer each question honestly by picking the option that best describes you. Take your time with each question. After you finish, add up your scores to see how well you fit as a central midfielder.

<u>**Assessment Questions:**</u>

Q. How comfortable are you in both defending and attacking, helping in all parts of the game?

a) I'm great at helping in both defense and attack from midfield.

b) I'm good at helping in both defense and attack.

c) I sometimes succeed in helping both defense and attack.

d) I find it hard to balance defending and attacking.

Q. How good are you at keeping the ball, passing it, and starting attacks?

a) I'm skilled at keeping the ball, passing it, and starting attacks.

b) I'm pretty good at keeping the ball, passing it, and starting attacks.

c) I'm okay at keeping the ball, passing it, and starting attacks.

d) I struggle with keeping the ball, passing it, and starting attacks.

Q. How well can you move across the field, making runs from one box to the other, and helping both defense and attack?

a) I'm excellent at covering the field, making runs, and supporting both defense and attack.

b) I'm good at moving across the field, making runs, and helping in both areas.

c) I sometimes manage to move across the field, make runs, and support both ends.

d) I find it hard to cover the field, make runs, and support both defense and attack.

Q. How comfortable are you in reading the game, predicting the play, and making key interceptions?

a) I'm great at reading the game, predicting the play, and making key interceptions.

b) I'm good at reading the game, predicting plays, and making interceptions sometimes.

c) I sometimes manage to read the game, predict plays, and make interceptions.

d) I find it hard to read the game, predict plays, and make interceptions.

<u>**Scoring and Results:**</u>

<u>**Give yourself points for each answer:**</u>

- a) = 4 points
- b) = 3 points
- c) = 2 points
- d) = 1 point

<u>**Add up your points to see how well you fit as a central midfielder:**</u>

12-16 points: You're a great fit to be a central midfielder. Keep working on your skills!

8-11 points: You're a good fit and have potential. Keep practicing!

4-7 points: You have some potential, but you might need to work on certain areas.

1-3 points: Central midfielder might not be the best position for you. You could explore other midfield roles.

<u>Remember, this assessment is a guide, and you can continue to grow and explore different positions in football.</u>

3. Attacking Midfielder (Playmaker) Assessment:

Are you thinking about becoming an attacking midfielder? This template will help you see if that's the right position for you based on your skills and qualities. Let's find out if you could be an attacking midfielder!

Instructions:

Answer each question honestly by picking the option that best describes you. Take your time with each question. After you finish, add up your points to see if you're a good fit as an attacking midfielder.

Assessment Questions:

Q. How comfortable are you with creating chances for goals and helping your teammates score?

a) I'm excellent at creating chances and providing assists.

b) I'm good at creating chances and providing assists sometimes.

c) I'm okay at creating chances and providing assists now and then.

d) I find it hard to create chances and provide assists.

Q. How good are you at finding open spaces, making smart runs, and taking advantage of gaps in the other team's defense?

a) I'm skilled at finding spaces, making smart runs, and using gaps in the defense.

b) I'm pretty good at finding spaces, making smart runs, and using gaps sometimes.

c) I'm okay at finding spaces, making runs, and using gaps in the defense.

d) I find it hard to find spaces, make runs, and use gaps effectively.

Q. How well can you control the pace of the game, direct play, and make key passes near the goal?

a) I'm great at controlling the game's pace, directing play, and making key passes.

b) I'm good at controlling the game's pace, directing play, and making key passes sometimes.

c) I'm okay at controlling the game, directing play, and making key passes now and then.

d) I find it hard to control the game's pace, direct play and make key passes.

Q. How comfortable are you with dribbling past opponents, taking on challenges, and creating space for yourself and others?

a) I'm excellent at dribbling past opponents, taking on challenges, and creating space.

b) I'm pretty good at dribbling, taking on challenges, and creating space sometimes.

c) I'm okay at dribbling past opponents and creating space now and then.

d) I struggle with dribbling, taking on challenges, and creating space.

<u>**Scoring and Results:**</u>

<u>**Give yourself points for each answer:**</u>

- a) = 4 points
- b) = 3 points
- c) = 2 points
- d) = 1 point

Add up your points to see how well you fit as an attacking midfielder:

12-16 points: You're a great fit for an attacking midfielder. Keep working on your skills!

8-11 points: You're a good fit and have potential. Keep practicing!

4-7 points: You have some potential, but you might need to work on certain areas.

1-3 points: Attacking a midfielder might not be the best position for you. You could explore other roles in the midfield.

<u>Remember, this assessment is a guide, and you can continue to grow and explore different positions in football.</u>

Template for Footballers: Finding Your Best Forward Position

1. Striker (Center Forward) Assessment:

Are you wondering if you have what it takes to be a striker? This guide will help you find out if being a center forward is the right position for you. Let's see if you're meant to be a striker!

Instructions:

Think about each question and pick the option that best matches your skills or what you prefer. Take your time and answer honestly. At the end, add up your points to see if you're a good fit as a striker.

Q. How confident are you in your ability to score goals regularly?

a) Very confident – I have a natural talent for scoring and can do it often.

b) Fairly confident – I can score often, but I still need to get better.

c) Somewhat confident – I score sometimes, but not as often as I'd like.

d) I am not confident; I find it hard to score regularly.

Q. How comfortable are you holding the ball, involving your teammates, and creating chances for them?

a) Very comfortable – I'm great at holding the ball, bringing in teammates, and creating chances for others.

b) Fairly comfortable – I can hold the ball and involve teammates, but I could improve.

c) Somewhat comfortable – I sometimes do well at holding the ball and involving teammates.

d) I am not comfortable. I struggle to hold the ball and involve my teammates effectively.

Q. How well can you make runs behind the defense, find open spaces, and time your movements to get through balls?

a) Excellent – I'm good at timing my runs and finding spaces to get through balls.

b) Good – I can make runs and find spaces, but I still need to get better.

c) Average – I sometimes make good runs and find spaces, but not always.

d) Poor – I have a hard time making effective runs and finding spaces.

Q. How comfortable are you with dribbling past defenders, using your speed and skill to create chances to score?

a) Very comfortable – I'm confident in dribbling past defenders and creating scoring chances.

b) Fairly comfortable – I can dribble past defenders, but I need to work on creating more chances.

c) Somewhat comfortable – I sometimes dribble past defenders and create chances.

d) Not comfortable – I struggle with dribbling past defenders and creating scoring chances.

<u>**Scoring and Results:**</u>

<u>**Give yourself points for each answer:**</u>

- a) = 4 points
- b) = 3 points
- c) = 2 points
- d) = 1 point

<u>**Add up your points to see how well you fit as a striker:**</u>

12-16 points: You're a great fit for a striker. Keep practicing and sharpening your skills!

8-11 points: You're a good fit and show promise. Keep working on improving!

4-7 points: You have potential, but you may need to work on some areas.

1-3 points: Striker might not be the best position for you. You could try exploring other roles as a forward.

2. Second Striker (Supporting Forward) Assessment:

Curious if you have what it takes to be a second striker? This simple guide will help you figure out if you're a good fit for the supporting forward role. Let's see if you're meant to be a second striker!

Instructions:

Think carefully about each question and choose the answer that best describes you. Take your time and be honest. When you're done, add up your points to see if you're a good fit as a second striker.

Assessment Questions:

Q. How comfortable are you with working closely with teammates, giving assists, and creating chances to score?

a) Very comfortable – I'm great at linking up with teammates and setting up scoring chances.

b) Fairly comfortable – I can work well with teammates and provide assists, but I could get better.

c) Somewhat comfortable – I sometimes do well linking up with teammates and creating chances.

d) Not comfortable – I find it hard to connect with teammates and set up assists.

Q. How well can you support the main striker, make smart runs, and get into good positions to receive passes?

a) Excellent – I'm good at timing my runs and helping the main striker effectively.

b) Good – I can support the main striker and make smart runs, but I still need to improve.

c) Average – I sometimes support the main striker well, but not always.

d) Poor – I struggle to help the main striker and make effective runs.

Q. How comfortable are you playing between the lines, finding open spaces, and connecting the midfield with the attack?

a) Very comfortable – I'm confident playing between the lines and linking up the midfield and attack.

b) Fairly comfortable – I can play between the lines, but I need to work on connecting the team better.

c) Somewhat comfortable – I sometimes play well between the lines and connect with the team.

d) Not comfortable – I find it hard to play between the lines and link up with the team.

Q. How well can you understand the game, spot chances, and make quick decisions to create scoring opportunities?

a) Excellent – I'm good at reading the game, spotting chances, and making quick decisions.

b) Good – I can read the game and spot chances, but I could improve my decision-making.

c) Average – I sometimes read the game well and spot chances, but not consistently.

d) Poor – I struggle to understand the game, spot chances, and make quick decisions.

<u>**Scoring and Results:**</u>

<u>**Give yourself points for each answer:**</u>

- a) = 4 points
- b) = 3 points
- c) = 2 points
- d) = 1 point

**<u>Add up your points to see how well you fit as a
second striker:</u>**

- **12-16 points:** You're a great fit for a second
  striker. Keep practicing and getting better!
- **8-11 points:** You have potential as a
  supporting forward. Keep working on your
  skills!
- **4-7 points:** You have some potential, but you
  might need to improve in certain areas.
- **1-3 points:** The second striker might not be
  the best role for you. You could try other
  forward positions.

**<u>Remember, this is just a guide, and you can always
grow and explore different positions as you
improve.</u>**

PART- 3

PERSONALIZED TRAINING
PLANS AND ROUTINES FOR
EVERY LEVEL

I want to give you a simple but very useful idea. Instead of trying to fit all your **nutrition plans, fitness programs, conditioning routines, techniques, and tools** inside this book, I encourage you to make your own **charts, tables, or posters** on a **big sheet of paper.**

Write down your **meal plans, workout schedules, key exercises, or important techniques** in a clear and organized way. Use different **colors, sections, or even images** if needed. Once done, **fix it on a wall**, **cupboard**, or any place where you can easily see it every day.

This way, you don't have to open the book again and again to check things. It will be **visible, easy to follow, and a great way to stay on track** with your football training and nutrition.

CHAPTER – 1

Custom Training Plans Based on Skill Level

Introduction:

In football, training should match the player's skill level so they can get better and perform well. This chapter gives training routines for beginners, intermediates, and advanced players. Each plan is designed to fit the player's level, with the right drills, exercises, and schedules to help them improve.

Section 1: Beginner Training Plan

Overview:

Beginners are usually new to football or don't have much experience. Their training plan is focused on learning basic skills, understanding the game, and building general fitness.

Goals:

- Learn basic football skills (dribbling, passing, shooting)

- Understand simple game tactics
- Get physically fit
- Build good training habits

Weekly Schedule:

Monday: Technical Skills and Ball Control

- **Warm-up:** Start with 10 minutes of jogging and stretching to get ready.
- **Dribbling drills:** Practice dribbling around cones and doing figure-eight dribbling for 20 minutes.
- **Passing drills:** Work on wall passes and passing with a partner for 20 minutes.
- **Shooting practice:** Spend 20 minutes practicing simple shots on goal.
- **Cool-down:** End with 10 minutes of stretching to relax your muscles.

Tuesday: Tactical Understanding and Small-Sided Games

- **Warm-up:** Begin with 10 minutes of jogging and stretching.
- **Introduction to tactics:** Learn about positions and formations for 20 minutes.
- **Small-sided games:** Play 3v3 or 4v4 games for 30 minutes.
- **Tactical drills:** Practice simple positioning and movement exercises for 20 minutes.
- **Cool-down:** Finish with 10 minutes of stretching.

<u>**Wednesday: Rest or Light Activity**</u>

- Take a break or do some light jogging or casual play to help your body recover.

<u>**Thursday: Physical Fitness and Conditioning**</u>

- **Warm-up:** Start with 10 minutes of jogging and stretching.
- **Agility drills:** Practice ladder drills and cone drills for 20 minutes to improve agility.
- **Endurance training:** Do interval running and shuttle runs for 20 minutes to build stamina.
- **Strength exercises:** Work on bodyweight squats, lunges, and push-ups for 20 minutes.
- **Cool-down:** End with 10 minutes of stretching.

<u>**Friday: Technical Skills and Ball Control**</u>

- Repeat Monday's routine but make small changes to keep things interesting.

<u>**Saturday: Friendly Match or Practice Game**</u>

- Play a friendly match or an organized practice game to use your skills in a real game.

<u>**Sunday: Rest or Recovery Activities**</u>

- Do some light stretching, yoga, or swimming to help your body recover and stay flexible.

Section 2: Intermediate Training Plan

Overview:

Intermediate players already know the basics of football and have some skills. This training plan helps them get better by adding more advanced drills and tactics.

Goals:

- Improve technical skills
- Learn more about tactics
- Get stronger and fitter
- Focus on playing in specific positions

Weekly Schedule:

Monday: Advanced Technical Skills

- **Warm-up:** Start with 10 minutes of stretching and light jogging to prepare your body.
- **Dribbling drills:** Practice advanced dribbling with cones and 1v1 situations for 20 minutes.
- **Passing drills:** Work on one-touch passing and triangle passing for 20 minutes.
- **Shooting practice:** Spend 20 minutes on target shooting and practicing volleys.
- **Cool-down:** Finish with 10 minutes of stretching to relax your muscles.

<u>**Tuesday: Tactical Training and Positional Play**</u>

- **Warm-up:** Begin with 10 minutes of stretching and light jogging.
- **Tactical drills:** Focus on defensive positioning and attacking patterns for 20 minutes.
- **Positional play:** Practice drills specific to your role on the field for 30 minutes.
- **Small-sided games:** Play 5v5 or 6v6 games for 20 minutes to apply tactics.
- **Cool-down:** End with 10 minutes of stretching.

<u>**Wednesday: Physical Conditioning and Strength Training**</u>

- **Warm-up:** Start with 10 minutes of stretching and light jogging.
- **Speed drills:** Do sprint intervals and exercises to improve acceleration for 20 minutes.
- **Strength training:** Focus on weight lifting like squats and deadlifts, and core exercises for 20 minutes.
- **Endurance training:** Run long distances or do fartlek training for 20 minutes to build stamina.
- **Cool-down:** Finish with 10 minutes of stretching.

<u>**Thursday: Rest or Active Recovery**</u>
- Do light activities like cycling, swimming, or gentle stretching to help your body recover.

Friday: Technical Skills and Tactical Drills

- Repeat the routines from Monday and Tuesday, but make small changes to keep things challenging.

Saturday: Full Match Simulation

- Participate in a full 11v11 match to practice game situations and use your tactical knowledge.

Sunday: Rest or Recovery Activities

- Engage in light stretching, yoga, or a gentle swim to help your body recover and stay flexible.

Section 3: Advanced Training Plan

Overview:

Advanced players are very skilled and have a deep understanding of football. This training plan helps them fine-tune their skills, learn advanced tactics, and reach their peak physical condition.

Goals:

- Perfect technical skills
- Deepen tactical knowledge and improve decision-making
- Reach the highest level of physical fitness
- Boost game intelligence and mental toughness

<u>Weekly Schedule:</u>

<u>Monday: Technical Mastery and Precision</u>

- **Warm-up:** Start with 10 minutes of dynamic stretching and intense warm-up drills.
- **Technical drills:** Focus on precise passing and advanced dribbling techniques for 20 minutes.
- **Shooting drills:** Practice power shots, finesse shots, and different shooting situations for 20 minutes.
- **Skills challenge:** Spend 20 minutes on free-kick practice and penalty kicks to sharpen your skills.
- **Cool-down:** End with 10 minutes of static stretching to relax your muscles.

<u>Tuesday: Tactical Intensity and Game Scenarios</u>

- **Warm-up:** Begin with 10 minutes of dynamic stretching and intense warm-up drills.
- **Tactical drills:** Work on high-press strategies and counter-attacking drills for 20 minutes.
- **Positional drills:** Practice role-specific scenarios and game simulations for 30 minutes.
- **Small-sided games:** Play 7v7 or 8v8 games with a focus on tactics for 20 minutes.
- **Cool-down:** Finish with 10 minutes of static stretching.

Wednesday: Peak Physical Conditioning

- **Warm-up:** Start with 10 minutes of dynamic stretching and intense warm-up drills.
- **Speed and agility:** Do advanced ladder drills and plyometrics for 20 minutes to improve quickness.
- **Strength training:** Spend 20 minutes on advanced weight lifting to build strength.
- **Endurance:** Focus on high-intensity interval training and stamina drills for 20 minutes.
- **Cool-down:** End with 10 minutes of static stretching.

Thursday: Rest or Active Recovery

- Do activities like foam rolling, yoga, or light jogging to help your body recover.

Friday: Technical and Tactical Reinforcement

- Combine the technical drills from Monday with the tactical scenarios from Tuesday for a complete session.

Saturday: Competitive Match Play
- Play in competitive matches or high-level scrimmages to apply your advanced skills and tactics in real-game situations.

Sunday: Rest or Recovery Activities
- Engage in light recovery activities to get ready for the next week of training.

CHAPTER – 2

Position-Specific Training Routines

Goalkeeper Training Routine:

Overview:
Goalkeepers need special training to get better at stopping shots, improving reflexes, and controlling the penalty area.

Goals:
- Get better at stopping shots and reacting quickly
- Improve positioning and decision-making
- Build physical strength and agility
- Develop communication and leadership skills

Weekly Schedule:

Monday: Shot-Stopping and Reflex Drills
- **Warm-up:** Start with 10 minutes of light jogging and stretching.

- **Shot-stopping drills:** Practice saving close-range shots and reacting to quick shots for 30 minutes.
- **Reflex drills:** Focus on quick reaction exercises for 20 minutes.
- **Positioning drills:** Work on 1v1 situations and handling crosses for 20 minutes.
- **Cool-down:** End with 10 minutes of stretching.

Tuesday: Distribution and Footwork

- **Warm-up:** Begin with 10 minutes of light jogging and stretching.
- **Footwork drills:** Practice ladder drills and cone exercises for 20 minutes to improve movement.
- **Distribution drills:** Work on throwing, kicking accuracy, and passing under pressure for 30 minutes.
- **Communication exercises:** Spend 20 minutes on commanding the defense and organizing set pieces.
- **Cool-down:** Finish with 10 minutes of stretching.

Wednesday: Physical Conditioning and Strength

- **Warm-up:** Start with 10 minutes of light jogging and stretching.
- **Strength training:** Do core exercises and upper body workouts for 20 minutes.

- **Agility drills:** Practice quick lateral movements and changes of direction for 20 minutes.
- **Endurance training:** Focus on interval running and shuttle runs for 20 minutes.
- **Cool-down:** End with 10 minutes of stretching.

Thursday: Rest or Active Recovery

- Engage in light activities like jogging, stretching, or yoga to help your body recover.

Friday: Game Scenarios and Situational Drills

- **Warm-up:** Begin with 10 minutes of light jogging and stretching.
- **Game scenarios:** Practice saving penalties and handling corner kicks for 30 minutes.
- **Situational drills:** Work on dealing with back passes and distributing under pressure for 30 minutes.
- **Cool-down:** Finish with 10 minutes of stretching.

Saturday: Match Simulation

- Participate in a full or half-field match to apply your skills in game-like situations.

Sunday: Rest or Recovery Activities

- Do light stretching, foam rolling, or swimming to help your body recover.

Defender Training Routine

Overview:

Defenders need to be great at tackling, positioning, and understanding the game to protect their goal and start attacks.

Goals:

- Get better at tackling and intercepting passes
- Improve positioning and awareness on the field
- Build physical strength and endurance
- Develop strong communication and teamwork

Weekly Schedule:

Monday: Tackling and Interception Drills

- **Warm-up:** Start with 10 minutes of light jogging and stretching.
- **Tackling drills:** Practice one-on-one defending and slide tackles for 30 minutes.
- **Interception drills:** Focus on anticipating and reading passes for 20 minutes.
- **Positioning drills:** Work on defensive formations and marking for 20 minutes.
- **Cool-down:** End with 10 minutes of stretching.

Tuesday: Passing and Ball Control

- **Warm-up:** Begin with 10 minutes of light jogging and stretching.

- **Passing drills:** Practice short passes, long passes, and switching play for 30 minutes.
- **Ball control drills:** Improve your first touch and receiving under pressure for 20 minutes.
- **Distribution exercises:** Work on clearing the ball and playing out from the back for 20 minutes.
- **Cool-down:** Finish with 10 minutes of stretching.

Wednesday: Physical Conditioning and Strength

- **Warm-up:** Start with 10 minutes of light jogging and stretching.
- **Strength training:** Do core exercises and lower body workouts for 20 minutes.
- **Agility drills:** Practice quick lateral movements and changes of direction for 20 minutes.
- **Endurance training:** Focus on long-distance running and interval training for 20 minutes.
- **Cool-down:** End with 10 minutes of stretching.

Thursday: Rest or Active Recovery

- Engage in light activities like jogging, stretching, or yoga to help your body recover.

Friday: Tactical Awareness and Communication
- **Warm-up:** Begin with 10 minutes of light jogging and stretching.

- **Tactical drills:** Practice defensive positioning and the offside trap for 30 minutes.
- **Communication exercises:** Spend 20 minutes organizing the back line and signaling movements.
- **Team drills:** Work on defensive teamwork and transitioning to attack for 20 minutes.
- **Cool-down:** Finish with 10 minutes of stretching.

Saturday: Match Simulation

- Participate in a full or half-field match to practice your skills in game-like situations.

Sunday: Rest or Recovery Activities

- Do light stretching, foam rolling, or swimming to help your body recover.

Midfielder Training Routine

Overview:

Midfielders need to be versatile. They should be good at both defending and attacking and must control the pace of the game.

Goals:

- Get better at ball control and accurate passing
- Improve vision and decision-making in the field
- Build physical endurance and strength

- Develop tactical awareness and proper positioning

Weekly Schedule:

Monday: Ball Control and Passing

- **Warm-up:** Start with 10 minutes of light jogging and stretching.
- **Ball control drills:** Practice dribbling in tight spaces and work on your first touch for 30 minutes.
- **Passing drills:** Focus on short passes, long passes, and through balls for 30 minutes.
- **Cool-down:** End with 10 minutes of stretching.

Tuesday: Tactical Awareness and Vision

- **Warm-up:** Begin with 10 minutes of light jogging and stretching.
- **Tactical drills:** Practice positioning and reading the game for 20 minutes.
- **Vision drills:** Work on peripheral vision and quick decision-making for 30 minutes.
- **Small-sided games:** Play 5v5 or 6v6 games for 20 minutes to practice tactical awareness.
- **Cool-down:** Finish with 10 minutes of stretching.

Wednesday: Physical Conditioning and Strength

- **Warm-up:** Start with 10 minutes of light jogging and stretching.

- **Strength training:** Do core exercises and lower body workouts for 20 minutes.
- **Agility drills:** Practice with ladder drills and cone drills for 20 minutes.
- **Endurance training:** Focus on interval running and long-distance running for 20 minutes.
- **Cool-down:** End with 10 minutes of stretching.

Thursday: Rest or Active Recovery

- Engage in light activities like jogging, stretching, or yoga to help your body recover.

Friday: Attack and Defence Balance

- **Warm-up:** Begin with 10 minutes of light jogging and stretching.
- **Defensive drills:** Practice tackling and intercepting for 20 minutes.
- **Attacking drills:** Work on shooting and creating chances for 20 minutes.
- **Transition drills:** Practice switching from defense to attack and vice versa for 20 minutes.
- **Cool-down:** Finish with 10 minutes of stretching.

Saturday: Match Simulation

- Participate in a full or half-field match to practice your skills in game-like situations.

<u>**Sunday: Rest or Recovery Activities**</u>

- Do light stretching, foam rolling, or swimming to help your body recover.

Forward Training Routine

<u>**Overview:**</u>

Forwards are the main goal scorers on the team. They need to be great at finishing, positioning, and creating chances to score.

<u>**Goals:**</u>

- Get better at finishing and shooting accurately
- Improve positioning and movement off the ball
- Build physical strength and agility
- Develop tactical awareness and creativity on the field

<u>**Weekly Schedule:**</u>

<u>**Monday: Finishing and Shooting**</u>

- **Warm-up:** Start with 10 minutes of light jogging and stretching.
- **Shooting drills:** Practice power shots, finesse shots, and volleys for 30 minutes.

- **Finishing drills:** Work on 1v1 situations with the goalkeeper and first-time finishes for 20 minutes.
- **Cool-down:** End with 10 minutes of stretching.

Tuesday: Positioning and Movement

- **Warm-up:** Begin with 10 minutes of light jogging and stretching.
- **Positioning drills:** Practice finding space and timing your runs for 20 minutes.
- **Movement drills:** Focus on making runs off the ball and creating angles for 20 minutes.
- **Small-sided games:** Play 5v5 or 6v6 games for 20 minutes to practice positioning and movement.
- **Cool-down:** Finish with 10 minutes of stretching.

Wednesday: Physical Conditioning and Strength

- **Warm-up:** Start with 10 minutes of light jogging and stretching.
- **Strength training:** Do core exercises and lower body workouts for 20 minutes.
- **Agility drills:** Practice lateral movements and sprint drills for 20 minutes.
- **Endurance training:** Focus on interval running and long-distance running for 20 minutes.
- **Cool-down:** End with 10 minutes of stretching.

<u>**Thursday: Rest or Active Recovery**</u>

- Engage in light activities like jogging, stretching, or yoga to help your body recover.

<u>**Friday: Creating and Converting Chances**</u>

- **Warm-up:** Begin with 10 minutes of light jogging and stretching.
- **Dribbling drills:** Practice beating defenders and close control for 20 minutes.
- **Chance creation drills:** Focus on crossing and making through balls for 20 minutes.
- **Finishing drills:** Work on converting crosses and quick shooting for 20 minutes.
- **Cool-down:** Finish with 10 minutes of stretching.

<u>**Saturday: Match Simulation**</u>

- Participate in a full or half-field match to practice your skills in real-game situations.

<u>**Sunday: Rest or Recovery Activities**</u>

- Do light stretching, foam rolling, or swimming to help your body recover.

CHAPTER – 3

Fitness and Conditioning Programs

Strength Training Program

Overview:

Strength training is important for building muscles, improving endurance, and preventing injuries. This plan focuses on making your core, upper body, and lower body stronger.

Goals:

- Make all your muscles stronger and more enduring
- Improve your core stability and balance
- Lower the chance of getting injured

Weekly Schedule:

Monday: Upper Body Strength

- **Warm-up:** Start with 10 minutes of light jogging and stretching.

- **Core exercises:** Do planks, Russian twists, and leg raises for 15 minutes.
- **Upper body exercises:** Practice push-ups, bench presses, and shoulder presses for 30 minutes.
- **Cool-down:** Finish with 10 minutes of stretching.

Tuesday: Lower Body Strength

- **Warm-up:** Begin with 10 minutes of light jogging and stretching.
- **Core exercises:** Do bicycle crunches, side planks, and mountain climbers for 15 minutes.
- **Lower body exercises:** Practice squats, lunges, and deadlifts for 30 minutes.
- **Cool-down:** End with 10 minutes of stretching.

Wednesday: Rest or Active Recovery

- Engage in light activities like jogging, stretching, or yoga to help your body recover.

Thursday: Full Body Strength

- **Warm-up:** Start with 10 minutes of light jogging and stretching.
- **Core exercises:** Do sit-ups, flutter kicks, and hollow holds for 15 minutes.
- **Full body exercises:** Practice burpees, kettlebell swings, and pull-ups for 30 minutes.
- **Cool-down:** Finish with 10 minutes of stretching.

Friday: Upper Body Strength
- Repeat Monday's routine.

Saturday: Lower Body Strength
- Repeat Tuesday's routine.

Sunday: Rest or Recovery Activities
- Do light stretching, foam rolling, or swimming to help your body recover.

Cardio and Endurance Program

Overview:
Cardio and endurance training are very important to keep your energy high and help you play well throughout the match. This plan includes exercises like running, interval training, and long-distance running.

Goals:
- Improve heart and lung fitness
- Build stamina and endurance
- Help your body recover faster

Weekly Schedule:

Monday: Aerobic Conditioning
- **Warm-up:** Start with 10 minutes of light jogging and stretching.
- **Aerobic exercises:** Do steady-state running, cycling, or swimming for 45 minutes.

- **Cool-down:** Finish with 10 minutes of stretching.

Tuesday: Interval Training

- **Warm-up:** Begin with 10 minutes of light jogging and stretching.
- **Interval exercises:** Do sprint intervals, running fast for 30 seconds and resting for 30 seconds, for 30 minutes.
- **Cool-down:** End with 10 minutes of stretching.

Wednesday: Long-Distance Running

- **Warm-up:** Start with 10 minutes of light jogging and stretching.
- **Long-distance run:** Run at a steady pace for 5-10 km, which should take about 45-60 minutes.
- **Cool-down:** Finish with 10 minutes of stretching.

Thursday: Rest or Active Recovery

- Do light activities like jogging, stretching, or yoga to help your body recover.

Friday: High-Intensity Interval Training (HIIT)

- **Warm-up:** Begin with 10 minutes of light jogging and stretching.
- **HIIT exercises:** Do exercises like burpees, jumping jacks, and high knees for 30 minutes.
- **Cool-down:** End with 10 minutes of stretching.

<u>**Saturday: Aerobic Conditioning**</u>
- Repeat Monday's routine.

<u>**Sunday: Rest or Recovery Activities**</u>
- Do light stretching, foam rolling, or swimming to help your body recover.

Speed and Agility Program

<u>**Overview:**</u>
Speed and agility training helps players become quicker, react faster, and move better. This plan includes exercises like ladder drills, cone drills, and jumping exercises.

<u>**Goals:**</u>
- Improve how fast you can start and reach your top speed
- Get better at changing direction quickly
- Develop better footwork and coordination

Weekly Schedule:

<u>**Monday: Ladder Drills**</u>

- **Warm-up:** Start with 10 minutes of light jogging and stretching.
- **Ladder drills:** Practice high knees, in-and-out steps, and side-to-side movements for 30 minutes.

- **Cool-down:** Finish with 10 minutes of stretching.

Tuesday: Cone Drills

- **Warm-up:** Begin with 10 minutes of light jogging and stretching.
- **Cone drills:** Do zig-zag runs, T-drills, and shuttle runs for 30 minutes.
- **Cool-down:** End with 10 minutes of stretching.

Wednesday: Plyometric Exercises

- **Warm-up:** Start with 10 minutes of light jogging and stretching.
- **Plyometric exercises:** Do box jumps, bounding, and skater hops for 30 minutes.
- **Cool-down:** Finish with 10 minutes of stretching.

Thursday: Rest or Active Recovery

- Do light activities like jogging, stretching, or yoga to help your body recover.

Friday: Speed Endurance

- **Warm-up:** Begin with 10 minutes of light jogging and stretching.
- **Speed endurance drills:** Run 100m and 200m sprints for 30 minutes.
- **Cool-down:** End with 10 minutes of stretching.

Saturday: Agility and Quickness Drills

- **Warm-up:** Start with 10 minutes of light jogging and stretching.
- **Agility drills:** Practice ladder drills and cone drills for 30 minutes.
- **Cool-down:** Finish with 10 minutes of stretching.

Sunday: Rest or Recovery Activities

- Do light stretching, foam rolling, or swimming to help your body recover.

CHAPTER – 4

Mental Conditioning and Visualization Techniques

Mental Toughness Exercises

Overview:

Mental toughness is about staying focused, confident, and strong when things get tough. Building mental toughness is important for handling pressure and keeping your performance high.

Goals:

- Improve focus and concentration
- Build resilience and never give up
- Increase confidence and belief in yourself

Exercises:

1. **Self-Talk:**
   - **Purpose:** Positive self-talk helps you feel more confident and motivated.

2. **<u>How to Practice:</u>**

- Notice when you have negative thoughts and try to replace them with positive ones.
- Examples of positive self-talk: "I am strong," "I can handle this," "I will succeed."

3. **<u>Goal Setting:</u>**

- **<u>Purpose:</u>** Setting clear and reachable goals keeps you motivated and focused.
- **<u>How to Practice:</u>**
    - Think about what you want to achieve in the short term and long term.
    - Make sure your goals are SMART (Specific, Measurable, Achievable, Relevant, Time-bound).
    - Regularly review your goals and adjust them if needed.

4. **<u>Stress Inoculation Training</u>**

- **<u>Purpose:</u>** Gradually getting used to stress helps you become more resilient.
- **<u>How to Practice:</u>**
    - Identify what stresses you out (like high-pressure games or hard training).
    - Gradually expose yourself to these stressors in a controlled way.

- Practice coping strategies like deep breathing or positive self-talk while facing these stressors.

5. **<u>Focus Drills:</u>**

   - **<u>Purpose:</u>** These drills help you improve your concentration and attention during games.
   - **<u>How to Practice:</u>**
     - Use concentration grids or focus apps to practice staying focused.
     - Try to focus on one task at a time without getting distracted, and gradually increase the time you spend on it.

<u>Visualization Practices</u>

<u>Overview:</u>

Visualization is about mentally practicing and imagining yourself playing well. It helps you improve your skills, feel more confident, and get ready for games.

<u>Goals:</u>

- Improve your skills and performance
- Build confidence and reduce nervousness
- Prepare your mind for upcoming games Practices

1. <u>**Daily Visualization Routine**</u>

- **Purpose:** Regular visualization helps you picture positive outcomes.
- **How to Practice:**
    - Set aside 10-15 minutes every day for visualization.
    - Find a quiet place, close your eyes, and relax.
    - Imagine yourself performing specific skills or playing in a game successfully.
    - Use all your senses—sight, sound, touch—to make the mental image as real as possible.

2. <u>**Pre-Game Visualization**</u>

- **Purpose:** Mentally get ready for the game ahead.
- **How to Practice:**
    - Before a game, spend some time visualizing key moments, like scoring a goal or making a save.
    - Focus on seeing yourself succeed in these moments.
    - Picture yourself handling any challenges calmly and confidently.

3. <u>**Skill-Specific Visualization**</u>

- **Purpose:** Use mental practice to improve a specific skill.

- **How to Practice:**
    - Pick a skill you want to get better at, like dribbling or passing.
    - Visualize yourself doing the skill perfectly in your mind.
    - Break the skill down into steps and mentally rehearse each one step by step.

Mindfulness Techniques

Overview:

Mindfulness is about being fully aware of the present moment without judging it. It helps players lower stress, stay focused, and manage their emotions better.

Goals:

- Lower stress and anxiety
- Improve focus and attention
- Better control over emotions

Techniques:

1. **Breathing Exercises:**

   - **Purpose:** Calm your mind and reduce stress by controlling your breathing.
   - **How to Practice:**
     - Practice deep breathing: Breathe in deeply through your nose, hold it for a few seconds, then slowly breathe out through your mouth.

- Try the 4-7-8 technique: Breathe in for 4 seconds, hold for 7 seconds, and breathe out for 8 seconds.
- Do these breathing exercises daily, especially before games or in stressful moments.

2. **<u>Body Scan Meditation:</u>**

- **Purpose:** Increase awareness of your body and help it relax.
- **How to Practice:**
    - Find a quiet place to sit or lie down comfortably.
    - Close your eyes and take a few deep breaths.
    - Slowly focus on each part of your body, from head to toe, noticing any tension or sensations.
    - Breathe deeply into the tense areas and try to relax them.

3. **<u>Mindful Walking:</u>**

- **Purpose:** Practice mindfulness while doing everyday activities.
- **How to Practice:**
    - Walk slowly and intentionally.
    - Pay attention to each step, the way your legs move, and how your feet touch the ground.

- Notice the sounds, smells, and sights around you without judging them.

4. **<u>Gratitude Journaling:</u>**

- **Purpose:** Focus on the good things in life to reduce negative thoughts.
- **How to Practice:**
    - Keep a daily journal.
    - Write down three things you are grateful for each day.
    - Regularly reflect on positive experiences and achievements.

CHAPTER – 5

Injury Prevention and Rehabilitation

Warm-Up and Cool-Down Routines

Overview:
Warming up properly before exercise helps get your blood flowing, makes your muscles more flexible, and gets your body ready to move, which helps prevent injuries. Cooling down after exercise helps your body recover and reduces muscle soreness.

Goals:
- Get your body ready for exercise
- Improve your performance
- Lower the chance of getting injured
- Help your body recover after exercise

Warm-Up Routine:

1. **General Warm-Up (5-10 minutes)**
   - **Purpose:** Raise your heart rate and get more blood to your muscles.

- **How to Perform:**
  - Start with light jogging or brisk walking for 5-10 minutes.
  - Gradually go faster to increase your heart rate.

2. **<u>Dynamic Stretching (5-10 minutes)</u>**

   - **Purpose:** Make your muscles more flexible and improve your range of motion.
   - **How to Perform:**
     - **Leg Swings:** Stand on one leg and swing the other leg forward and backward, then side to side. Repeat with the other leg.
     - **Arm Circles:** Stretch your arms out to the sides and make small circles, gradually making them bigger.
     - **Walking Lunges:** Step forward with one leg, lower your hips, and bend both knees to 90 degrees. Switch legs and repeat.
     - **High Knees:** Jog in place, lifting your knees up toward your chest with each step.

3. **<u>Sport-Specific Drills (5-10 minutes)</u>**

   - **Purpose:** Get your body ready for the specific movements in football.
   - **How to Perform:**

- **Dribbling Drills:** Practice
  dribbling a football, focusing
  on control and quick
  movements.
- **Passing Drills:** Pair up with a
  teammate and pass the ball
  back and forth.
- **Sprinting Drills:** Do short
  sprints to mimic game
  situations.

Cool-Down Routine:

1. **Light Aerobic Exercise (5-10 minutes)**

   - **Purpose:** Gradually bring your heart
     rate down and prevent blood from
     pooling in your legs.
   - **How to Perform:**
     - Do light jogging or brisk
       walking for 5-10 minutes.

2. **Static Stretching (5-10 minutes)**

   - **Purpose:** Increase your flexibility and
     reduce muscle stiffness.
   - **How to Perform:**
     - **Hamstring Stretch:** Sit on the
       ground with your legs straight
       out in front of you, and reach
       forward to touch your toes.

- **Quadriceps Stretch:** Stand on one leg, and pull the other foot up toward your buttocks.
- **Calf Stretch:** Stand facing a wall, place one foot back, and press your heel into the ground.
- **Shoulder Stretch:** Extend one arm across your body, and use your other arm to pull it closer.

Flexibility & Mobility Exercises

Overview:

Keeping your body flexible and mobile is important for staying injury-free and performing well. Doing these exercises regularly helps keep your joints healthy and your muscles loose.

Goals:

- Make it easier for your body to move in different directions
- Keep your muscles stretchy and flexible
- Help prevent injuries

Exercises:

1. **Foam Rolling (5-10 minutes)**
   - **Purpose:** Ease tight muscles and improve blood flow.
   - **How to Perform:**

- **Quadriceps Roll:** Lie face down with a foam roller under your thighs. Roll from your hips to your knees.
- **IT Band Roll:** Lie on your side with a foam roller under your outer thigh. Roll from your hip to your knee.
- **Back Roll:** Lie on your back with a foam roller under your spine. Roll from your upper back to your lower back.

2. **<u>Dynamic Stretching (5-10 minutes)</u>**

- **Purpose:** Get your body ready to move.
- **How to Perform:**
    - **Leg Swings:** Stand on one leg and swing the other leg forward and backward, then side to side. Do this for both legs.
    - **Arm Circles:** Stretch your arms out to the sides and make small circles, gradually making them bigger.
    - **Hip Circles:** Stand with your feet shoulder-width apart, and rotate your hips in a circular motion.

3. **<u>Static Stretching (5-10 minutes)</u>**

- **Purpose:** Keep your muscles flexible and prevent them from getting tight.

- **How to Perform:**
- **Hamstring Stretch:** Sit on the ground with your legs straight out in front of you, and reach forward to touch your toes.
- **Quadriceps Stretch:** Stand on one leg and pull the other foot up toward your buttocks.
- **Calf Stretch:** Stand facing a wall, place one foot back, and press your heel into the ground.
- **Shoulder Stretch:** Extend one arm across your body, and use your other arm to pull it closer.

4. **<u>Mobility Drills (5-10 minutes)</u>**

- **Purpose:** Improve how well your joints move.
- **How to Perform:**
    - **Hip Openers:** Stand with your feet shoulder-width apart, lift one knee up and out to the side, then lower it back down. Switch legs.
    - **Thoracic Rotations:** Sit on the ground with your legs stretched out, place one hand behind your back, and rotate your upper body to the opposite side. Alternate sides.
    - **Ankle Circles:** Sit on the ground with your legs extended, and rotate your ankles in a circular motion.

CHAPTER – 6

Templates and Tools Section

Overview:

This section gives you important templates and tools that can help you improve as a football player. You can use these to check your skills, track how you're doing, set goals, plan your meals, and manage your recovery. These resources are here to help you become a better player.

Skill Assessment Checklists

Purpose:

Skill assessment checklists let you check how good you are at different parts of your game. They help you see where you're strong and where you need to get better. By knowing this, you can make a training plan that focuses on improving the areas you need the most help with.

1. Technical Skills Checklist

Dribbling: [ ] Excellent [ ] Good [ ] Needs Improvement

Passing: [ ] Excellent [ ] Good [ ] Needs Improvement

Shooting: [ ] Excellent [ ] Good [ ] Needs Improvement

Ball Control: [ ] Excellent [ ] Good [ ] Needs Improvement

Tackling: [ ] Excellent [ ] Good [ ] Needs Improvement

2. Tactical Skills Checklist

Positioning: [ ] Excellent [ ] Good [ ] Needs Improvement

Game Awareness: [ ] Excellent [ ] Good [ ] Needs Improvement

Decision Making: [ ] Excellent [ ] Good [ ] Needs Improvement

Defensive Skills: [ ] Excellent [ ] Good [ ] Needs Improvement

Offensive Skills: [ ] Excellent [ ] Good [ ] Needs Improvement

3. **<u>Physical Skills Checklist</u>**

Speed: [ ] Excellent [ ] Good [ ] Needs Improvement

Agility: [ ] Excellent [ ] Good [ ] Needs Improvement

Strength: [ ] Excellent [ ] Good [ ] Needs Improvement

Endurance: [ ] Excellent [ ] Good [ ] Needs Improvement

Flexibility: [ ] Excellent [ ] Good [ ] Needs Improvement

4. **<u>Mental Skills Checklist</u>**

Focus: [ ] Excellent [ ] Good [ ] Needs Improvement

Confidence: [ ] Excellent [ ] Good [ ] Needs Improvement

Stress Management: [ ] Excellent [ ] Good [ ] Needs Improvement

Motivation: [ ] Excellent [ ] Good [ ] Needs Improvement

Teamwork: [ ] Excellent [ ] Good [ ] Needs Improvement

<u>Weekly Training Log</u>

<u>Purpose:</u>

A weekly training log helps you keep track of what you do in training, see how you're improving, and make changes to your routine if needed.

<u>Template:</u>

<u>Weekly Training Log:</u>

Day	Training Activity	Duration	Intensity Level (1-10)
Monday			
Tuesday			
Wednesday			
Thursday			
Friday			
Saturday			
Sunday			

Note: make it on any big paper/chart/sheet.

Goal-Setting Worksheets

Purpose:

Goal-setting worksheets help players define their short-term and long-term goals, create actionable plans, and stay motivated to achieve their objectives.

Template:

Goal-Setting Worksheet

1. **Long-Term Goals**

Goal 1:

____

Goal 2:

____

Goal 3:

____

2. **Short-Term Goals:**

Goal 1:

____

Goal 2:

____

Goal 3:

____

3. **<u>Action Plan:</u>**

Steps to Achieve Long-Term Goal 1:_______________

Steps to Achieve Long-Term Goal 2:_______________

Steps to Achieve Long-Term Goal 3:_______________

Steps to Achieve Short-Term Goal 1: _______________

Steps to Achieve Short-Term Goal 2: _______________

Steps to Achieve Short-Term Goal 3: _______________

4. **<u>Progress Tracking:</u>**

Date: _______________ | Goal: _______________ |

Progress:

____

Date: _______________ | Goal: _______________ |

Progress:

____

Date: _______________ | Goal: _______________ |

Progress:

____

Nutrition and Meal Planning Templates

Purpose:

Proper nutrition is essential for peak performance. Nutrition and meal planning templates help players create balanced diets that meet their energy needs and support their training and recovery.

Template:

Nutrition and Meal Planning Template

1. **Daily Meal Plan**

Breakfast:

____

Mid-Morning Snack:

____

Lunch:

____

Afternoon Snack:

____

Dinner:

____

Evening Snack:

____

2. **Weekly Meal Planner**

Day	Breakfast	Snack 1	Lunch	Snack 2	Dinner	Snack 3
Monday						
Tuesday						
Wednesday						
Thursday						
Friday						
Saturday						
Sunday						

Note: make it on any big paper/chart/sheet.

Recovery and Rest Day Schedules

Purpose:

Rest and recovery are important for healing muscles and staying in top shape. A recovery and rest day schedule help you plan your rest times and activities to stay strong and avoid getting hurt.

Recovery and Rest Day Schedule

1. ## Weekly Recovery Schedule

   Monday: Light stretching and foam rolling

   Tuesday: Active recovery (light swimming or cycling)

   Wednesday: Rest day (complete rest)

   Thursday: Light yoga or stretching

   Friday: Active recovery (light walking or jogging)

   Saturday: Rest day (complete rest)

   Sunday: Light stretching and foam rolling

2. ## Recovery Activities

   Stretching:

   ____

   Foam Rolling:

   ____

Massage:

____

Hydration:

____

Nutrition:

____

3. **<u>Sleep Schedule</u>**

Bedtime: _______________________________

Wake-Up Time: ___________________________

PART- 4

"OBSTACLES &
CHALLENGESIN THE
PATH OF FOOTBALL
PLAYERS & INDIAN
FOOTBALL PROGRESS"

<u>Financial constraints, with many players coming from low-income backgrounds</u>

For many football players from low-income families, money can be a big challenge. They might struggle to afford basic things like football boots and pads. Even the fees for joining teams or leagues can be too high. Getting to and from practices and games can also be tough if transportation costs are too high. This makes it harder for some kids to participate fully.

Playing on elite or club-level teams is often more expensive, and these teams might have higher fees and more practice. This can be a burden for families with less money. Additionally, players from low-income families may not have access to private coaching or special training like those from wealthier backgrounds. This can limit their growth and development as players.

CLARIFICATION

Although many football players from low-income families face financial challenges, many efforts and organizations are working to make football more accessible for them. These include scholarships, financial aid programs, and equipment donation drives. Some teams and leagues also offer reduced or waived fees for players who need help.

HOW TO OVERCOME

Here are some ways to support players from low-income backgrounds:

- **Provide financial help** to cover living costs while they pursue football.
- **Partner with local businesses** to offer financial support to these players.
- **Organize fundraisers** to raise money for player development.

- **Offer scholarships** to talented athletes from low-income families.
- **Set up a mentoring program** to guide and support these players.
- **Create a network of coaches and volunteers** in the community to train them.
- **Help with transportation** to and from practices and games.
- **Raise awareness** of the challenges faced by these players and gather support through social media and other platforms.

CHAPTER – 2

<u>LIMITED SUPPORT FOR WOMEN'S FOOTBALL IN INDIA</u>

There are several reasons why women's football in India has not received much support.

One reason is cultural. In India, which has a traditionally patriarchal society, women's sports are often seen as less important than men's sports. Female athletes are not given the same respect as male athletes, making it harder for women's football to gain acceptance and support.

Another big reason is the lack of visibility and media attention. The media in India has not focused much on women's football, making it difficult for the sport to grow and attract fans.

There is also a lack of investment in the sport. Football, whether played by men or women, is not very popular in India, so there hasn't been much money put into it by either the government or private companies. Because of this, women's football has fewer facilities and hasn't been able to grow as fast as it could.

Finally, the lack of positive role models and successful teams has made it hard to attract young women to the sport. Without strong women's teams and players to look up to, it's been challenging to create excitement and interest in football among young girls.

The lack of interest in women's football in India is due to a mix of societal, cultural, and financial reasons. However, there has been some progress in recent years. The government and private organizations have started to show more interest in the sport. India's national women's team has participated in a few international competitions, and some clubs have started investing in women's teams. This positive trend is expected to keep improving in the coming years.

HOW TO OVERCOME

1. Increase funding for women's football programs and teams.
2. Give female players the same pay and benefits as male players.
3. Get more media coverage and promotion for women's football in India.
4. Build a strong youth program to attract and keep young talent.
5. Encourage more girls to play football from a young age.
6. Improve the quality of facilities and equipment for women's teams.
7. Start a professional league for women's football in India.
8. Partner with organizations that support and promote women's sports.
9. Increase the number of female coaches and referees in football.
10. Encourage more corporate sponsors to help grow the sport.

CHAPTER – 3

The limited scope of professional football as a career option in India

The scope of professional football as a career in India is limited for several reasons. One big issue is the lack of good facilities and infrastructure. Football has not been as popular in India as other sports, so the government and private companies haven't invested much in it. Without proper training grounds and playing facilities, it's hard for professional teams to perform well, and young players don't get the chance to improve their skills.

Another reason is the absence of a strong professional league system. Unlike other countries, where football leagues are well-established and give players a clear path to becoming professionals, India's domestic league system is less developed. This makes it tough for young players to find opportunities to play at a professional level, and clubs struggle to attract and retain talent.

A weak national team is also a problem. Success in international tournaments can raise the popularity of the sport and open up chances for players to join foreign leagues. However, the Indian national team has faced difficulties on the global stage, which makes young players less motivated to pursue football as a career.

Cultural factors play a role too. Cricket is the most popular sport in India, and most aspiring athletes choose to pursue cricket professionally. This makes it harder for football to attract the best talent, and players find it tough to earn a living through football.

In India, teams and players also don't have access to stable finances or good investment opportunities. Because of this, many players may not be able to build a long-term career in football, as clubs often face financial difficulties. The lower pay and fewer benefits for professional football players in India, compared to other countries, may also stop young players from choosing football as a career.

The limited career options in professional football in India are due to a mix of issues, like lack of proper organization, cultural factors, and weak infrastructure. However, with football becoming more popular and efforts being made to improve the domestic league, the future looks better for professional football in the country.

HOW TO OVERCOME

1. Professional football teams and leagues in India should get more money to improve the level of play and bring in more talented players.
2. Build a good youth development program to find and keep young talent.
3. Increase media coverage and promotion of professional football in India to make more people aware and interested in the sport.
4. Start a strong professional football league in India where players can show their skills and attract teams and sponsors.
5. Improve the quality of training facilities and equipment for professional teams and players.
6. Get more companies to sponsor professional football to help teams grow.
7. Partner with groups that support and promote professional football in India.
8. Make it easier for amateur players to move up and play professional football.
9. Start more programs to scout and find young players with talent.
10. Encourage more organizations to invest in developing young football players.

CHAPTER – 4

Lacking Football culture in certain areas

Cricket has been played in India for a long time and is the most popular sport in the country. Even though football is loved worldwide, it hasn't gained the same success in some Indian states like Madhya Pradesh, Rajasthan, Uttar Pradesh, Chhattisgarh, and Bihar.

One reason for this is the lack of resources and infrastructure in these areas. These states are not as developed as others, so they do not spend as much on sports training or facilities. This means that young people from these regions don't have the same chances to develop their football skills or think of football as a career.

Another reason is the lack of exposure and role models. In areas where cricket is more popular, young people may not know much about football or see it as an option because it doesn't get much attention in the media. Since there isn't a strong football tradition in these places, there are fewer football players for young people to look up to and be inspired by.

Also, the lack of professional football leagues and clubs in these regions plays a role. Without a professional team or league, it's harder for people in these areas to get excited or become fans of football.

CLARIFICATION

There are many reasons why football hasn't grown much in some parts of India. These include not enough exposure to the sport, few resources, and a lack of role models. Cricket is more popular and the absence of professional football leagues and clubs also plays a big role. To help football grow in these areas, it's important to build better facilities, give young people more chances to learn and play and promote the sport more through media and strong role models.

HOW TO OVERCOME

1. Build more football fields and stadiums in areas where football is not popular.
2. Start football teams and leagues in local communities and schools to get more people playing.
3. Invest in programs that help young players improve their skills.
4. Increase media coverage of football games and events to raise awareness and get people interested.
5. Host international football matches in India to bring more attention to the sport.
6. Give more girls and women the chance to play football and compete at higher levels.
7. Use social media to share highlights, content, and news about upcoming games to attract more fans.
8. Organize football training sessions and invite professional players to lead these sessions for all age groups.
9. Provide financial help and support to local football teams so they can grow and improve.
10. Invest in building a strong national football team that can compete internationally and help promote the sport in India.

CHAPTER – 5

A lack of government support for Football

Football in India doesn't get as much government funding as other sports for several reasons.

One reason is that football has fewer fans than cricket, which is India's most popular sport. Because of this, the government may focus more on funding cricket and other sports with bigger fan bases.

Another reason is that the Indian football team hasn't had the same international success as the cricket team. The national football team hasn't played in as many big international tournaments, so it may not receive as much funding. Also, because the public is more interested in cricket, football gets less attention and support.

In some parts of India, a lack of resources and sports facilities also limits support for football. These areas are less developed, so they don't invest as much in sports, including football. This means young people in these regions have fewer chances to improve their skills and pursue football careers compared to those in more developed areas.

Finally, the All India Football Federation (AIFF), which manages football in India, has faced issues with how it is run. Problems in the AIFF have led to the government having less trust in the organization, further reducing support for football.

There are several reasons why football in India doesn't get enough government support. Cricket is the most popular sport, so it gets more attention and funding. Football hasn't had much success in international tournaments, which also affects the level of support it gets. The public is more interested in cricket, making it harder for football to gain attention.

Another issue is the lack of good leadership and transparency in the body that manages Indian football, the AIFF. This causes the government to trust football less and give it less support.

For football to receive more help, it needs to grow in popularity, have better facilities, succeed internationally, and be managed with honesty and good leadership.

HOW TO OVERCOME

1. Start a football development program funded by the government. The government can provide money to help grow football in India by building new facilities, supporting youth programs, and promoting the sport overall.
2. Encourage corporate sponsorship. The government can ask companies to sponsor football teams and leagues, which will bring in more money for the sport.
3. Work with the media to increase coverage of football. The government can team up with TV and news outlets to show more games and events, making more people interested in football.
4. Help plan international football events. The government can organize and host international football matches and tournaments to get more people excited about the sport.
5. Support the creation of a professional football league. The government can help provide money and resources to teams, clubs, and players to make football more professional in India.

CHAPTER – 6

Lack of proper nutrition and dietary guidance for players

Indian football players, like many athletes in developing countries, often face problems with food and diet. One big reason is that many players come from poor families and cannot afford healthy food or a personal dietitian to guide them.

Another issue is the lack of knowledge about how eating healthy affects performance. Many players may not know how to eat the right food to keep their bodies strong for training and matches.

Cultural food habits also play a role. Many Indian players might stick to traditional diets, which may not provide enough protein or other nutrients needed to recover and build muscles.

The problem gets worse because players often don't have access to proper training facilities, especially in villages or small towns. Without these facilities, it becomes even harder to focus on eating the right food.

Lastly, there isn't enough help from coaches or team managers. Teams often don't have enough money to hire dietitians, and most coaches don't have the knowledge to guide players about food and nutrition properly.

CLARIFICATION

To improve the food and diet of Indian football players, we need to teach players, coaches, and teams why eating healthy is so important for better performance. This can be done through workshops, classes, and simple training sessions. Teams and players should also get help like money, good facilities, and personal diet experts to make sure they eat the right food and stay in top form.

HOW TO OVERCOME

- Hire a good food expert to make a meal plan for each player.

- Teach players why eating healthy food is important for playing well.

- Make sure players get healthy food during practice and matches.

- Add foods like fruits, vegetables, lean meat, and whole grains to their meals.

- A good diet should have enough protein, carbs, and healthy fats.

- Encourage players to eat small meals often to keep their energy high all day.

- Explain what to eat before and after playing to stay strong and recover better.

- Check players' weight and fitness and change their meals if needed.

- Avoid junk food, sugary snacks, and sweet drinks.

CHAPTER – 7

Societal pressure to pursue other career paths

The pressure from society can strongly affect if someone wants to choose football as a career. In many cultures, like in India, people value education and traditional jobs like becoming a doctor, engineer, or business person. Parents and families often think football is risky and doesn't have a secure future, so they don't support it.

Another reason is the lack of proper facilities and professional leagues in India. Without good places to train or play, it becomes hard for young players to improve and show their talent. This makes it tough for them to earn a living through football, which stops many from taking it seriously as a career.

Also, football is not very popular in the Indian media, so young players don't have many local heroes to look up to. Without seeing successful Indian football players, they can't imagine themselves becoming professional players.

Money is another big issue. Many football players in India can't earn enough to live comfortably. They often have to do other jobs to support their families, leaving them less time to train and compete. This makes it harder for them to stay committed to the sport.

Lastly, there's not enough support for young players. Many people think football isn't a real career choice. Because of this mindset, young players often lose motivation and struggle to stay focused on their dreams.

Football needs to be encouraged and supported more so that people see it as a good career choice. To do this, young players should be given more chances to improve and show their skills. There should also be more focus on Indian football in the media, and successful Indian players' stories should be shared to inspire others.

Football players need better financial support so they can fully focus on training and playing without worrying about money. This can help them perform at their best.

It is also important to change how society views football and encourage young talent to follow their dreams in the sport. Indian football players have the talent and passion to do well. With the right facilities, leagues, and support, they can have successful careers and earn a good living through football.

- Start your football journey by setting clear and simple goals for yourself.

- Understand that pressure from society is common and not just for football players. Many successful people have faced it too.

- Surround yourself with people who believe in you and support your dreams.

- Be ready to work hard to improve your football skills and build strong discipline.

- Stay focused on your goals, even when things don't go as planned or you face challenges.

- Look for opportunities to learn about football, like joining youth programs or taking part in events related to the sport.

- Be open to learning new things and listen to advice from coaches, mentors, and experienced people in football.

- Remember, becoming a professional football player takes time and patience. Success doesn't happen overnight.

- Always stay confident in yourself and think positively about your abilities.

- Choose a career that makes you happy, and don't let others decide your path for you.

CHAPTER – 8

Racial bias in the Indian football system

Racial bias in Indian football means unfair treatment of players because of their background, race, or where they come from. This can show up in different ways, like giving fewer chances to certain players, treating them unfairly, or not supporting them enough. It also includes not having enough players from these groups in the top levels of football.

One example is the lack of players from the north-eastern states on the national team. Even though many talented players and football fans come from these states, they are often ignored when picking players for the national team. These areas don't have proper facilities or enough support for football, and players from these states face unfair treatment and bias.

Another example is players from the Indian diaspora, especially those of African descent. These players often face racism and unfair treatment in football. They are not given many opportunities and struggle to find their place in the sport.

This problem isn't limited to players. Coaches and administrators also face racial bias. For example, there are many talented African coaches in India, but very few of them get jobs in Indian football. This is because they face discrimination and don't get equal opportunities in the system.

When players from underrepresented backgrounds don't get fair chances, they can't show their full potential. This not only affects the players but also hurts the growth of football in India. It limits the talent available for the national team and slows down the progress of the sport in the country.

CLARIFICATION

To fix racial bias in Indian football, we need to work together to fight unfair treatment and discrimination. This means improving football facilities and support in areas that don't have enough, giving more chances to players from ignored communities, and encouraging diversity and equality in the sport.

The Indian Football Association and other groups in charge must put in serious effort to make football fair for everyone. They can do this by training players and coaches about these issues, focusing on football development in areas that are left out, and making sure there is better diversity in leadership roles within the sport.

Racial bias is a big problem in Indian football, and it needs to be addressed to help the sport grow and ensure every player gets a fair chance to succeed. By taking steps to end discrimination and encourage equality, Indian football can become a place where all players feel included and treated fairly.

HOW TO OVERCOME

- Add more leaders from ignored racial groups in Indian football organizations.

- Make sure players from all backgrounds get the same chances to join professional teams and youth programs.

- Increase diversity among coaches, referees, and other football-related jobs in India.

- Teach players, coaches, and officials about the harm caused by racism and how to stop it.

- Speak out against racist behavior by fans and promote a welcoming culture.
- Work with groups that fight for equality and inclusion in sports.
- Keep track of and address cases of racism in Indian football and hold people and organizations responsible.
- Celebrate and highlight the success of players from ignored racial groups.
- Regularly check and improve the plans and policies created to fight racism in Indian football.
- Provide support and help to players and others who face racism in the football system.

CHAPTER – 9

Language and cultural barriers in Indian football

Indian football has grown a lot in recent years. The Indian Super League (ISL) has gained popularity. However, despite these good changes, the sport still faces some problems because of different languages and cultures.

One big challenge is the lack of a common language among players. The Indian national team includes players from different regions, and each region has its own language and way of speaking. This can cause problems with communication and teamwork on the field. English is the official language for football in India, but many players find it hard to understand and use.

Another problem is the players' different cultural backgrounds. India is a country with many cultures, each having its own traditions and customs. These cultural differences can sometimes lead to misunderstandings or disagreements among players, which can hurt the team's mood and performance.

To solve this, the ISL and Indian football teams are working on hiring coaches who speak different languages and choosing players carefully. This helps reduce language problems and makes it easier for players to communicate well on the field.

CLARIFICATION

In some parts of India, people don't show much interest in football. This is another cultural problem. Cricket is the most loved sport in many regions, and football doesn't get the same support or resources. Because of this, talented football players from these areas find it hard to make it to the national team or professional leagues.

The Indian football team is trying to solve this problem by promoting the game in different parts of the country. They are also bringing in foreign players to make the game more exciting and popular.

Language and cultural problems are still big challenges for Indian football. But efforts are being made to overcome these issues. By supporting more languages and understanding different cultures, Indian football is moving towards creating a better and more united football culture. With these steps, Indian football can grow stronger and achieve great things.

- Hire coaches who can speak different languages, including local ones, to help players communicate better.
- Provide language classes for players and staff to make communication easier.
- Create an environment where every player feels welcomed, no matter what language they speak or where they come from.
- Encourage players to share their cultural stories and experiences with their teammates.
- Build a team culture that respects and values differences among players and staff.
- Organize cultural exchange programs for players and coaches to learn from one another.
- Plan team activities that promote teamwork and understanding among everyone.
- Use translators for important messages to ensure everyone understands clearly.
- Set up a support team to help players and staff who face problems with language or cultural differences.
- Allow players and staff to openly share their concerns and ideas about language or cultural issues, and listen to them carefully.

CHAPTER – 10

Insufficient number of professional clubs

India does not have enough professional football clubs, which is a big problem for the growth of football in the country. Even though football is becoming more popular, players don't have enough chances to improve their game or build a career because there are not enough professional clubs.

One main reason for this is the lack of money being invested in football. Cricket is much more popular in India, so sponsors and investors prefer to put their money there instead of football. Also, India doesn't have strong league systems, good facilities, or proper infrastructure, which scares many potential investors.

Another issue is that India doesn't have a clear and organized league system. Right now, there are many leagues and tournaments running at the same time, which makes it hard for players to build their careers and for clubs to gain recognition. Without a proper structure, it's also difficult for clubs to attract and keep good players, as many players prefer to join better-organized leagues.

India also doesn't have enough proper infrastructure for football, like good training grounds, academies, or stadiums. Without these, it becomes harder for clubs to host matches, organize events, and attract talented players.

CLARIFICATION

Football in India needs more money and a proper league system to fix these problems. The government can help by building better facilities and offering benefits to private companies that invest in football. At the same time, efforts should be made to make the game more popular and grow a strong fan base. This will help attract more sponsors and investors who can support the sport.

Even though football is becoming more loved in India, not having enough professional clubs is a big challenge for the game's growth. To solve this, it's important to deal with the lack of money, the confusing league system, and the shortage of good facilities. Only then can football grow and become a bigger part of India's sports culture.

HOW TO OVERCOME

- The government should give more money to football teams and build better facilities.
- Private companies should be encouraged to invest in football clubs.
- Focus more on programs that help kids and young players learn football.
- Make football more popular by showing it more on TV and in the news.
- Start a proper league system like the ones in Europe.
- Allow more foreign players in the league to attract talent and improve the game.
- Improve the quality of coaching and build better training centers.
- Organize more matches with teams from other countries to help players learn different playing styles.
- Motivate businesses to sponsor football teams and leagues.
- Make football easier to play and enjoy by using online tools and involving local communities in the sport.

CHAPTER – 11

Lack of proper infrastructure for football

A big problem stopping football from growing in India is the lack of proper facilities. Without the right tools and places to train, it's hard for players to improve their skills, for clubs to find and keep good players, and for the game to become popular all over the country.

One major issue is the lack of good training centers and academies. Many young players don't have access to proper training places, good equipment, or skilled coaches. This makes it hard for them to practice, improve, and move forward in their football careers. Also, because there aren't enough professional academies and youth programs, players miss out on learning from experienced coaches and getting noticed by big teams.

Another problem is the poor condition of stadiums and other places for matches. Many stadiums in India are old and not well-maintained. They don't have enough seats or proper facilities for players and fans. This makes it tough for clubs to organize games, attract crowds, or earn money from events.

CLARIFICATION

The lack of good facilities and proper infrastructure also makes it hard for India to host big international football tournaments. Hosting such events could help football grow in the country and bring more money into the economy.

To fix these problems, India needs to invest in building and improving football facilities. This means creating and maintaining good training centers, academies, and stadiums. The government could provide money for these projects, and private investors could also be encouraged to help by offering financial benefits. Along with this, promoting football and building a strong fan base is important to attract more sponsors and investors who can support the sport.

India's poor football infrastructure is a big challenge for the sport's growth in the country. Without proper training centers, academies, and good stadiums, teams and players cannot improve or compete at a high level. Improving these facilities is key to making football stronger in India and helping the game reach more people.

HOW TO OVERCOME

- **<u>Government help:</u>** The government can give money and support to improve football facilities in India.

- **<u>Attract private investors:</u>** Offer tax benefits and other rewards to encourage private companies to invest in football infrastructure.

- **<u>Focus on young players:</u>** Start strong programs at the local level to find and train young talented players.

- **<u>Build modern training centers:</u>** Create advanced training facilities for both players and coaches to help them improve their skills.

- **<u>Better stadiums:</u>** Build new stadiums and upgrade old ones to meet international standards, making them suitable for big matches.

- **<u>Partner with foreign clubs:</u>** Work with football clubs and organizations from other countries to share knowledge and resources.

- **<u>Use technology:</u>** Bring in tools and techniques to improve player training, coaching methods, and overall management of football.

- **<u>Promote the game:</u>** Use media and community events to create more interest and excitement around football.

- **<u>Start youth leagues:</u>** Organize leagues for young players to give them more chances to play and grow in the sport.

- **<u>Build professional leagues:</u>** Create strong professional leagues where players can showcase their talent and attract top talent to Indian football.

CHAPTER – 12

Limited access to professional football coaching in India

Professional football coaching is not very common in India because of several reasons. One big reason is the lack of proper football facilities and infrastructure. Many football fields and stadiums in India are in bad condition and are not good enough for proper training or professional matches.

Another problem is the shortage of skilled and experienced coaches. Many coaches in India don't have the right training or experience to teach professional players, which makes it hard for athletes to improve.

Football in India also doesn't get enough money or support. Both the government and private companies spend very little on football compared to other sports like cricket. This means that clubs and academies don't have enough money to hire good coaches, buy quality equipment, or create good training spaces.

Lastly, the league system in India is not very strong. The Indian Super League (ISL) is the main football league, but it doesn't have the same level of competition or structure as famous leagues in Europe or South America. This makes it harder for players and coaches to grow and show their talent.

CLARIFICATION

India doesn't have enough proper football facilities, skilled and experienced coaches, money, or a strong football culture. These are the main reasons why professional football coaching is not easily available in the country.

To improve football in India, both the government and private companies need to spend money on better league systems, good coaches, and proper facilities.

HOW TO OVERCOME

- Use online resources like training videos, tutorials, and courses to help you learn on your own.

- Connect with players or coaches from other countries through social media or online forums to understand different coaching styles and techniques.
- Join local football teams or leagues to improve your skills and get some real experience.
- Attend football camps or workshops organized by international coaches in India.
- Look for chances to train with experienced coaches in India and make the most of them.
- Find academies or courses that focus on teaching and developing football players in detail.
- Use tools like footballs, cones, and agility ladders to practice and improve your fitness and skills.
- Take advantage of India's growing love for football to meet other players and coaches who share the same passion.
- Talk to players and coaches who have overcome the challenges of limited coaching in India and learn from their experience.
- Keep learning by reading about football, watching matches, and staying updated about the sport.

CHAPTER – 13

Limited access to modern football training equipment

A big problem for football in India is that players don't have access to modern training equipment. Good tools and technology are very important to train professional players, but most football clubs and academies in India don't have them.

One of the main reasons for this is a lack of money. Football doesn't have as many fans in India, so it doesn't get enough money from the government or private sponsors. Because of this, clubs and academies find it hard to buy the training tools they need.

Another reason is the poor condition of infrastructure. Many football fields and stadiums in India are not well-maintained, which makes it hard for players to practice and play properly. Also, many clubs and academies don't have proper places to store or take care of the equipment they have, so it quickly becomes old and useless.

CLARIFICATION

India's lack of modern football training equipment is a big reason why the sport is not growing much. To improve football in the country, the government and private companies need to spend money on better fields, good tools, and skilled coaches. This will help clubs and academies provide players and coaches with the right equipment to train better and perform at a higher level.

HOW TO OVERCOME

- Practice in open spaces like parks or playgrounds for drills and exercises.
- Use simple things like plastic bottles to make cones or other training tools at home.
- Share equipment with friends or local teams during group training sessions.

- Find groups that donate football equipment to communities that need help.

- Check with nearby football teams or academies to see if you can use their equipment.

- Look for local government programs that provide sports equipment to poor areas.

- Use online training videos and courses to learn and practice without much equipment.

- Join local tournaments or matches where equipment is provided for the event.

- Try to raise money for equipment through sponsors, grants, or crowdfunding.

- Buy tools that are simple, reliable, and can be used for many types of training.

CHAPTER – 14

Limited financial support for Indian football players

Indian football has a long history and a big fan following, but it still struggles to get enough money and become more popular. This is because of several reasons like not enough support from the government, lack of good facilities, and low investment in the sport.

One big problem is that football players in India don't get enough money. Many players have to do other jobs to take care of their families because they can't earn enough from football alone. This makes it hard for them to focus on their training and perform well. Also, young talented players may not want to choose football as a career because there isn't much financial reward in it.

The government has also been criticized for not doing enough to help Indian football grow. Even though football is loved by many and has potential, the government hasn't spent enough money on building better facilities or giving financial help to teams and players. Because of this, football in India struggles to compete with other sports and to gain recognition at the global level.

CLARIFICATION

Indian football has struggled to get enough money and become more popular in recent years. The main reasons for this are the lack of financial support for players, not enough investment in facilities, and very little help from the government. These problems have slowed down the growth of football in India. To help Indian football reach its full potential and become important on the world stage, these issues need to be fixed.

HOW TO OVERCOME

- Increase government help for football: The government can give money to help teams and players get better and play at higher levels.
- Get more companies to sponsor: Businesses can support teams and players by giving them the money they need to succeed.

- Add more teams and leagues: With more professional teams and leagues, players will have more chances to earn money through sponsorships and other deals.
- Make football more popular: If more people like football, more fans will come to games, which will bring in more money for teams and players.
- Start programs for kids: Create programs to encourage kids to play football, which will bring in more talented players for the future.
- Build better facilities: New stadiums and practice fields will make it easier for players and teams to improve their skills and play better.
- Allow private owners for teams: Let businesses or people own teams, so there's more money to support players and teams.
- Pay players better: Higher salaries will attract talented players, which will improve the quality of the game.
- Focus on youth training: Teach kids and teenagers more about football, so they grow into skilled players and make the sport stronger.
- Play in more global events: Competing internationally will make Indian football more famous and bring in more sponsors to help players and teams.

CHAPTER – 15

Limited Medical and Sports science support for Indian football players

Indian football players face big problems because they don't get enough medical care or sports science support. Without proper medical help, players can get injured more easily and take longer to recover. This can hurt their performance on the field and even shorten their careers.

Another issue is the lack of sports science tools like good diet plans, fitness training, and proper exercise routines. Sports science can help players stay in better shape, avoid injuries, and perform well during games. Without these things, it becomes harder for players to compete at the highest level, and they may never reach their full potential.

This problem is even worse for young players. To improve their skills and grow into great footballers, young athletes need medical care and sports science support. Without this help, it's harder for them to get better quickly and achieve their best as players.

One big problem Indian football players face is the lack of proper medical care and sports science support. This can seriously affect their health and how well they perform on the field. Without good medical care, players may get injured more often and take longer to recover, which can slow down their progress.

CLARIFICATION

To help Indian football grow and become a strong force globally, it's very important for the country to invest in better medical care and sports science support for its players. This will not only improve their performance but also help them stay fit and play at their best.

HOW TO OVERCOME

- Provide more money for research on how to improve Indian football players' performance and keep them from getting injured.

- Hire experienced doctors and sports science experts to help the national team and local football clubs.
- Check all players' health regularly to find and fix any problems early.
- Design special programs to prevent injuries that match the specific needs of Indian football players.
- Work with well-known sports medicine centers to get access to advanced tools and expert advice.
- Use data to track how players perform and manage injury details to make better decisions for their health.
- Encourage football organizations to hire their own medical staff and build proper facilities.
- Build a strong network of sports trainers, physiotherapists, and masseurs to support players across the country.
- Keep a record of every player's medical history and have a plan ready to help injured players recover.
- Train coaches and staff so they understand more about sports medicine and can use it to help players.

CHAPTER – 16

Limited scouting and recruitment opportunities for Indian football players

Indian football players face big problems because there aren't enough chances for them to get noticed and hired by professional teams. Without a proper system to find and recruit players, many talented footballers don't get the chance to show what they can do. This holds them back from reaching their full potential and becoming the footballers they are capable of being.

One major reason for this issue is the lack of proper facilities and resources for scouting and recruitment. In many places in India, scouting and hiring systems are not well-funded or well-organized. Because of this, it becomes harder for teams to find and sign talented players. On top of that, many scouts and teams focus only on players from big or well-known leagues, while ignoring those from smaller or less-famous teams and leagues.

Another big issue is that Indian players don't get enough exposure. Many of them don't have the chance to play in international matches or tournaments, which makes it harder for professional teams to notice them. Without this exposure, Indian players struggle to compete with players from other countries for contracts with professional teams.

CLARIFICATION

The lack of scouting and recruitment opportunities is a big challenge for Indian football players. The main reasons behind this problem are the poor scouting system, not enough resources and facilities, and limited chances for Indian players to get noticed. Without proper scouting, it becomes hard to find and support talented players, stopping them from reaching their best and competing at higher levels.

To solve this, Indian football needs to focus on building a better system to spot and recruit players. This will help discover new talent, support their growth, and give them the chance to perform at the top level. By investing in such a system, more players can be given the right opportunities to shine and prove themselves on the big stage.

- Increase money to help with finding players and scouting in parts of India that don't get enough attention.
- Work with local football clubs and academies to find and train talented young players.
- Use tools like videos and data tracking to discover talented players even from faraway places.
- Create one big database where all Indian players' details can be stored to help clubs and coaches spot new talent.
- Start more professional football clubs in India to give players more chances to play at a higher level.
- Offer rewards to clubs that invest in finding new players and helping young players grow.
- Organize talent-hunt events across India to find and promote new young players.
- Arrange more matches between Indian teams and teams from other countries so players get more experience and visibility.
- Build a good training program for coaches so they can teach better, especially at the beginner levels.
- Support young Indian players to play in famous foreign leagues.

Unavailability of quality football fields and proper maintenance in India

The poor condition of football fields and lack of proper care is a big problem for Indian football. Many football fields in India are not well-maintained and do not have basic features like good drainage systems, watering facilities, or proper lights. This makes it hard for players to practice and play at a good level. It also increases the chances of games being canceled because the fields are not in good condition. When fields are not taken care of, they get worse over time and can even cause players to get hurt. This affects not only the performance of players but also the growth of football in the country.

Bad football fields also make it harder for teams to bring in fans and sponsors, which hurts the sport's financial support. On top of that, it limits opportunities for young players to improve their skills and reduces chances for local people to enjoy and participate in the game.

Football fields need to be improved and taken care of regularly by both the government and private companies. This can be done by building new football stadiums, fixing up old ones, and providing money to keep the fields in good condition. With better fields, players will have a good place to train and play, which will help improve the quality of Indian football.

CLARIFICATION

The poor condition of football fields is a big issue for Indian football. It affects not only how players perform but also the overall growth of the sport in the country. To improve football in India, both the government and private companies should work together to develop and maintain better football fields. This will give players a proper place to practice and compete, which will help the sport grow.

HOW TO OVERCOME

- **Government support:** The government can help by building and taking care of good football fields in schools and local areas.
- **Help from private companies:** Businesses can also pay for building and maintaining football fields, especially in cities.
- **Community efforts:** People in the community can come together to improve and take care of their local football fields by volunteering or raising money.
- **Spreading awareness:** Teaching people why it's important to look after football fields can encourage them and organizations to take responsibility for keeping the fields in good condition.
- **Working with local clubs:** Joining hands with local football clubs and organizations can help get funds and materials to keep fields in great shape.

CHAPTER – 18

Limited opportunities to play in international competitions for Indian football players

The Indian national football team has not done much in international competitions. There are many reasons for this, like poor facilities, no strong league system across the country, and not enough support for the sport at the grassroots level.

Because of this, Indian players don't get many chances to show their talent or gain experience on the world stage. Since 1950, the national team has not made it to the World Cup and has always had a low FIFA ranking.

Indian clubs also struggle in the Asian Football Confederation Champions League. Without playing more international matches, Indian players find it hard to improve their skills or get noticed by big clubs and other national teams.

CLARIFICATION

The government and private organizations need to put more money into improving football facilities and building a strong league system in India. This will give Indian players more chances to play against top teams and improve their skills.

HOW TO OVERCOME

- Put more money into improving local football leagues and building better football facilities to raise the level of Indian football.

- Invite foreign teams to play friendly matches in India to give Indian players more experience.

- Send Indian teams to more international tournaments to help them learn and grow.

- Work with foreign clubs and academies so Indian players can get training and exposure.

- Find talented players at a young age and train them to make a strong national team.

- The government should give more money to help grow football in the country.

- Start a professional league system that will attract top players from around the world to come and play in India.

- Give Indian football more coverage in the media to get more people interested and excited about it.

- Start a program to train young players from the grassroots level and help them improve.

- Offer rewards to clubs and organizations that focus on training and developing young players.

Politics, Nepotism, And Corruption Have Been Significant Problems In Indian Football

For many years, Indian football has faced big problems like politics, favoritism, and corruption. These problems have made it hard for the sport to grow, causing trouble for players, coaches, and fans.

Corruption is one of the biggest issues in Indian football. There have been many cases of match-fixing, illegal betting, and bribes given to players and officials. This kind of corruption not only damages the name of Indian football but also makes the game unfair for everyone involved.

Favouritism, or nepotism, is another big problem. Jobs like coaching and managing are often given to people because of personal connections, not because they are skilled or experienced. This means unqualified people end up in important roles, which slows down the progress of football in the country.

Politics also causes major trouble in Indian football. Political leaders often interfere in decisions, and many officials are chosen because they care more about their own careers than the future of the sport. This leads to a lack of honesty and responsibility, making it harder for football to grow and improve.

These problems don't just affect the sport itself. They also hurt the players who dream of fair opportunities and the fans who want a game that is honest and transparent.

CLARIFICATION

To fix the problems of corruption, favouritism, and politics in Indian football, serious efforts are needed. There should be strict punishments for those involved in corruption or favouritism, stronger rules, and better monitoring to make sure the game is run fairly. Football needs to be more open and honest so that everyone involved feels confident in the system.

It's also important to focus on young players and fans. Grassroots programs should be promoted, and proper facilities should be built to support the growth of football at the local level. Offering more coaching and training programs for young players can help them develop their skills. Spreading awareness and building interest in football can also bring in more support for the game.

The government and the governing body for football in India, AIFF, need to work together to create clear rules for the game. These rules must be strictly followed to ensure football in India has a strong and fair foundation. This can create a better environment for football to grow and succeed in the long run.

HOW TO OVERCOME

- Football organizations should follow strict rules for keeping records of their money and checking them regularly. This will make sure everything is clear and fair.
- A new group should be set up to manage football in India and make sure all rules are followed properly.
- Clear rules should be made for hiring, firing, and promoting players, coaches, and managers so that only the most deserving people get the job.
- A proper program should be started to find young talented players and help them improve their skills.

- Businesses and people who put money into football should get tax benefits and other rewards to encourage private investment in the sport.
- More women and girls should be encouraged to play football by supporting programs specially designed for them.
- New stadiums and training centers should be built, and old ones should be upgraded to improve football facilities in India.
- Football can become more popular if matches are shown on TV and if more money is spent on advertising and promoting the game.
- Strong rules should be made to stop corruption in football, and those who break these rules should face strict punishment.
- Players, coaches, and managers should be taught to value honesty, respect, and teamwork to create a culture of fair play and good sportsmanship.

Lack Of Post-Retirement Support For Football Players

In India, football players face big problems after they retire. Once they stop playing, many players find it hard to earn money and often have to depend on themselves to take care of their families. This becomes a major struggle, especially for players who didn't get a chance to earn a lot of money during their careers.

One main reason for this problem is that India doesn't have a proper pension system for football players. Unlike in some other sports, retired football players in India don't get any pension or financial support from the government or football leagues. This makes it difficult for them to manage their expenses and take care of their families.

Another issue is that retired football players don't have enough job opportunities. Many players don't have formal education or skills that they can use outside of football, which makes it hard for them to find jobs. On top of that, some players struggle to adjust to life without football and feel lost, not knowing what to do next.

Retired Indian football players need more help and support to manage their lives after football. There should be job training programs, job placement opportunities, and a proper pension system for them. These steps can make it easier for players to earn a living after their careers end.

Players should also get counseling and other support services to help them adjust to life without football. This can guide them in finding new goals and staying positive.

Not having enough support after retirement is a big problem for Indian football players. Giving them better help will allow them to live comfortably and even contribute to society in new ways once they stop playing.

HOW TO OVERCOME

- **Learning to manage money**: Football players should learn how to save money and plan for life after retirement. This will help them secure their future.
- **Exploring other jobs**: Players should be encouraged to think about other careers while they are still playing football, so they have another option when their playing days are over.
- **Health care**: Football players need proper medical care during and after their careers to treat injuries or health problems caused by playing the sport.
- **Mental health support**: Football players should have access to comprehensive medical support and treatment both during their playing careers and after retirement to manage injuries and other health conditions that may have been brought on or made worse by their careers.
- **Social support and activities**: Retired players should have chances to meet others, take part in social events, and build a sense of belonging. This can help them feel less lonely and make their retirement journey smoother.

Lack of media coverage and exposure for Indian football

Even though India has a huge population and millions of football fans, the sport does not get enough media attention. One big reason for this is the strong influence of cricket. In India, cricket is not just a sport; it feels like a religion. It gets most of the media coverage, sponsorships, and money, leaving little space for football and other sports to grow.

Another reason why Indian football does not get much media attention is that people see the national team and local leagues as weak. Right now, the Indian football team is ranked 103rd in the world, and the local leagues have not produced many successful international teams. Because of this, there is not much excitement or interest in Indian football.

Football in India also has many problems with how it is managed. The All India Football Federation (AIFF), which controls football in the country, has been criticized for not being open about its decisions and not taking responsibility for its actions. People have also blamed AIFF for not doing enough to develop football at the grassroots level and promote the game properly.

CLARIFICATION

Even with these problems, there are some signs that Indian football is getting better. Since it started in 2014, the Indian Super League (ISL) has made football more popular and improved the level of competition in the country. The ISL has also brought in some foreign players, which has helped more people take an interest in Indian football.

The Indian football team has also shown improvement in recent years. The team has regularly won the SAFF Championship and performed well in the World Cup qualifying matches.

There are also private efforts to promote football in India. Many private clubs, academies, and schools have started investing in the sport. This can help football become more popular and also improve the skills of young players.

HOW TO OVERCOME

- **<u>Make a strong football league:</u>** A good league in India can bring more fans and give Indian players a better chance to show their skills.

- **<u>Improve the quality of the game:</u>** By investing in better stadiums, good coaches, and proper training, Indian football can get better, which will attract more fans and media.

- **<u>Focus on young players:</u>** If more kids play football from a young age, they will develop a love for the game, and more people will want to play in the future.

- **<u>Bring in foreign players:</u>** Letting foreign players join Indian leagues can make the matches more exciting, which will bring in more fans and media attention.

- **<u>Build a strong online presence:</u>** Indian football should use social media, websites, and online streaming to reach more people and gain more coverage.

- **<u>Work with media channels:</u>** If football organizations work with TV channels, newspapers, and websites, football will get more media attention.

- **<u>Host big tournaments:</u>** Hosting events like the FIFA World Cup or the AFC Asian Cup can help Indian football get noticed around the world.
- **<u>Get celebrities involved:</u>** If famous people and social media influencers talk about football, more people will start paying attention to the game.
- **<u>Show Indian players' achievements:</u>** When Indian footballers do well in India or other countries, their success should be highlighted so more people take an interest in the sport.
- **<u>Put more money into football:</u>** The government and private companies should invest more money in better stadiums, training, and youth programs to help the sport grow.

<u>Thank You</u>

"Thank you for reading this book. It means a lot that you took the time to go through these pages. I really appreciate your interest and hope this book gave you something useful to think about. If it helped you see things in a new way, then that makes me truly happy. Keep learning, keep asking questions, and always stand up for what is right. I wish you success in everything you do and hope you find happiness and strength in your journey. Stay motivated, keep believing in yourself, and never stop moving forward."